HOMELESS YOUNG PEOPLE IN BRITAIN

THE CONTRIBUTION OF THE VOLUNTARY SECTOR

written for ERICA and DSU by
Barbara Saunders

with cartoons by Peter Kneebone

Published in association with
ERICA and DSU by
BEDFORD SQUARE PRESS | NCVO

Published by the
Bedford Square Press of the
National Council for Voluntary Organisations
26 Bedford Square, London WC1B 3HU

© ERICA and DSU, 1986

ISBN 0 7199 1171 0

Printed in Great Britain by Biddles of Guildford

CONTENTS

European Research into Consumer Affairs (ERICA)

ERICA is a registered charity whose aim is to conduct research, resulting in action, for the benefit of consumers in all the countries of the European Community. It is concerned with all consumers but is particularly interested in the problems of the underprivileged. ERICA has produced reports on schemes to help disabled people get around independently. It has published *How to Start a Dial-a-Ride* and *Grants for Europe: How to get money and influence policy* (3rd edition, Bedford Square Press, 1986).

The hallmarks of ERICA'S work are:

- that it investigates problems of concern to all Europe's consumers
- that it aims to find solutions which can be put into practice immediately
- that it uses the experiences of one country to help others
- that it seeks those solutions which provide maximum benefit at the least possible cost

ERICA's core-funding was provided by the Consumers' Association (UK), but funds for individual research projects have to be obtained from other sources, private or public.

Disabilities Study Unit (DSU)

DSU is a trust for social welfare studies and research. Founded 10 years ago, it seeks to promote research into the problems of disabled people and of the socially disadvantaged and the ways in which their special needs can be met. The wide-ranging reports published by DSU include studies of child health and welfare services in many parts of the world, facilities for the disabled in sports centres and arts centres, rehabilitation studies, legislative guides, and consideration of disablement within the family.

1
INTRODUCTION:
Aims and Methodology

The United Nations Children's Fund (UNICEF) estimates that there are 70–80 million homeless young people in urban areas throughout the world and that their numbers are swelling by 5 million a year. While most of these – 40 million – are in Latin America, there are 20 million in Asia, 10 million in Africa, and it is estimated that there are 10 million abandoned children in the industrially developed countries.

A crisis of enormous proportions has arisen around the world. But while it is particularly evident in the 'barrios' of Brazil, in the slums of Bogotá and on the streets of other Third World cities, voluntary organisations are also highlighting homelessness among the young as a significant issue in the cities of the developed world. Experts suggest that there are at least 500,000 homeless youth in the United States and that as many as 20,000 sleep rough on the streets of New York every night. Information about these children and young people is hopelessly inadequate and, in the absence of reliable data, dependent to a large extent on anecdotal reports.

International concern for the plight of street children was expressed during the International Year of the Child (1979). Concern was translated into action in 1982 when a group of international non-governmental organisations (NGOs) affiliated to the United Nations and interested individuals launched the 'Inter-NGO Programme on Street Children and Street Youth'. Members included UNICEF, International Save the Children, the International Catholic Child Bureau, and the World Council of Churches. Their aims were broadly:

- To share information and experience among those working with street children.
- To raise the level of public awareness about street children.
- To improve existing programmes, facilitate fund-raising and propose national and international policies, programmes and legislation to ease the plight, and help overcome the tragedy, of street children.

The Inter-NGO Programme ceased to exist in 1985 but some of the founders are preparing to set up a new organisation to continue the work. They plan research, seminars and information sheets which will be of practical use to field workers.

Duncan Guthrie, a UK representative on the Inter-NGO Programme and Director of DSU, realised that too little was known about the needs of street youth for an effective response to be made. The number of homeless young people world-wide seemed to be increasing rapidly and an appropriate response was called for. Without it, the numbers of young people on the streets vulnerable to exploitation, crime, violence and prostitution will inevitably continue to rise. Talks took place between DSU and ERICA, focusing on the situation nearer home.

The UK Pilot Project

ERICA and DSU planned to analyse the situation in countries of the European Community and consider appropriate recommendations. The present report describes a pilot project, which studies the work being done by concerned agencies in Great Britain and is the first phase of a more extensive European study. A European Young Homelessness Group was established in Strasbourg in 1985. It aims to raise the profile of homelessness as a European issue and obtain European Community funds for projects to help young people. As a result of the Group's work a draft resolution was drawn up, but lost prominence when it was incorporated in a report to the European Parliament on Child Abuse – the Peus Report – which was adopted in January 1986. The Group is continuing to press for a resolution specifically on young people's housing and for the Commission to support a study of young homelessness throughout the Community. It will identify examples of the most effective means of helping homeless young people, enabling agencies working in this field to learn from each others' experiences.

The terms of reference for this first phase of the European research are:

- To carry out a study of the facilities for homeless young people provided by government agencies and voluntary organisations in England, Scotland and Wales.

- To investigate their current policies, working methods, plans for the future and sources of funding.

- To consider the perceived characteristics of the homeless young people for whom the agencies cater, the age groups involved, the reasons, real or alleged, for their homelessness and their personal attitudes to their situation.

In a short-term project, over three months, it was not possible to fulfil all those terms of reference. That would require a much lengthier enquiry. Priorities identified were to look at ways in which different voluntary organisations responded to the needs of homeless young people, to analyse the strengths and weaknesses of particular projects as perceived by the workers and to identify elements which may assist anyone working in the field or wishing to be involved, both in the UK and in due course in other European countries.

Nor was it possible to provide a comprehensive assessment of street youth, their characteristics, needs and available provision. This report describes what is happening on the ground in a number of towns and cities in Britain, the issues of concern to those who are working with young people and the action they feel is necessary to improve their quality of life.

The report is based on informal interviewing of staff and project workers on site between October and December 1985 and is supported by documentary analysis of published materials such as annual reports, and statistical data. Thirty-two organisations were visited and telephone conversations and written material obtained from a further 15 (Appendix 1). A wide range of voluntary organisations, both national and local, were visited. They included hostels, day centres, housing associations and street-based projects. Many of the projects carried out a variety of activities and offered a range of services including, for example, a day centre, short-stay accommodation, a coffee bar, medical facilities. A brief description of the projects visited is included in Appendix 2.

Initially this research aimed to look at the response of voluntary organisations to street youth in the cities of Britain. It soon became clear that the issues were much broader and the problems not confined to the cities. So interesting projects were studied wherever they occurred within the time constraints.

Lack of time also ruled out independent analysis of particular public issues, such as the impact of the Board and Lodging Regulations, or the need to amend the legislation relating to housing for young people. The responses express the views of the organisations visited and give a clear indication of the trends and needs which have implications for policy makers. The similarity of their views about future policy makes it possible for ERICA and DSU to be confident in their recommendations.

Voluntary projects are characterised by inadequate resources and highly committed but insufficient staffing. ERICA and DSU are very grateful to all who gave freely of their limited time to participate in this analysis. People working with local projects who were not part of national networks particularly valued the opportunity to share their knowledge. Because of the pressures under which they work, they tend to be unable to release staff to participate in co-ordinating committees (where they exist) and felt isolated from what was happening in the rest of the country.

2
STREET YOUTH IN BRITAIN:
An Overview

The Hidden Homeless

Street children are characterised by the lack or poor quality of housing, unemployment, poverty and malnutrition. They receive little affection and suffer from the diseases which are the inevitable consequence of a street-based life, poor housing and an inadequate diet. On the fringes of society and often, too, on the fringes of the economy, they eke out a marginal existence, learning to live on their wits and to follow the esoteric rules, customs and vocabulary that go with street life. Often friendless, they are considered to be a nuisance rather than young people in need or the victims of an uncaring society.

With the exception of London, there are not large numbers of young people in Britain living permanently on the streets, developing their own sub-cultures, acquiring the skills necessary to survive outside the legal and institutional framework, as in Naples, Bogotá or Bombay. The climate, even during the summer, militates against a street-based existence. The Vagrancy Act 1824, makes it an offence to beg in a public place. People 'wandering abroad' can be prosecuted if they fail to apply for accommodation at a reasonably accessible place of shelter (free of charge) to which they are directed; while under Section 64 of the Metropolitan Police Act 1839 people can be taken into custody if they are found between sunset and 8 a.m. 'lying or loitering in any highway, yard or other place and not giving a satisfactory account of themselves'. The system of Supplementary Benefit is also funda-

5

mental since it makes payments largely dependent on having a roof over one's head.

Although at the present time Britain does not have a large young, street-based population, there is a rapidly increasing number of homeless young people who find themselves trapped in a downward spiral of homelessness, unemployment and social deprivation which can end with life on the streets.

On the whole Britain through its legislation has effectively removed the down-and-outs from the city streets, courtyards and alleyways. In their place are 'the hidden homeless', without family support or a home of their own, dependent for a roof on the vagaries of the housing market; for income on Supplementary Benefit. They are consigned to a life in low-standard, high-cost bed-and-breakfast establishments, hostels and emergency night shelters. For these young people, every so often the strain of finding and keeping a roof over their heads becomes too much, and they sleep rough. A random sample of 307 young people from 16 to 19 in Livingston, Scotland in 1983 showed 20 per cent had slept rough and 60 per cent of those had been in care. *Centrepoint*, an emergency night shelter in Soho, London which accommodates 2,000 young people a year, estimates that one third of its residents have slept rough or in squats. *Shades* advice centre in Manchester considers that in the summer this is often preferable to bed-and-breakfast at the bottom end of the range.

No one knows the point at which young people give up the search for accommodation and consign themselves to the streets. It will vary from individual to individual, but it signifies the bottom line. The housing record of many young people in Britain today is characterised by temporary stays in different types of accommodation, periods of sleeping on the floor with friends, a return to the family or a relative which breaks down and consigns them back to the streets, tramping between agencies until another temporary solution is found.

Young people in Britain do not suffer the fate of being born and brought up on the streets like their Asian, Mediterranean or Latin American counterparts. They are not '*of* the street'

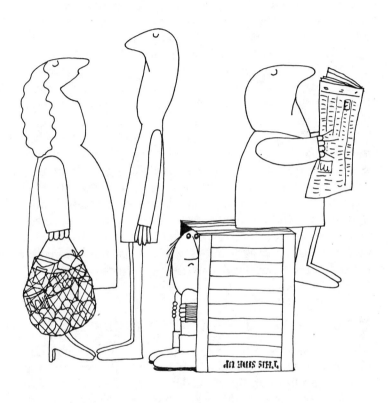

THIS SIDE UP

7

in that sense but find themselves '*on* the streets', sleeping rough or in short-stay temporary accommodation, unemployed, wandering aimlessly during the daytime, disenfranchised and unable to influence authorities at this most crucial and impressionable stage of their lives. Each phase on the streets may leave them more damaged, but also more 'streetwise' than the previous experience. Some will have no prospect of an improvement in their life-style in the longer term. This is hardly appropriate for young people in the 1980s. The street life in Britain's cities is not glamorous. It is isolated, unfriendly and largely uncaring. It exploits the natural credulity of young people and increases their vulnerability.

A myth has grown up, and continues to be fostered by the media, that young people follow Dick Whittington on the trail to London, seeking streets paved with gold. It bears little relation to the reality. A minority are genuinely attracted to London and other cities for work, the bright lights and any opportunity that presents itself. Except for these few, the problem of street children in Britain does not have its origins in the cities, although that is where it is most publicly exhibited. Street youth in Britain is a phenomenon from beyond the city limits.

Public Attitudes to Homelessness

Moving away from home to establish an independent household is a perfectly normal development in the transition from youth to adulthood. But nowadays most young people expect to make this transition earlier than previously and are increasingly unwilling to suffer the tensions of living at home once they reach the age of majority. Some do not have the option of staying within a family because they have been in care, or because breakdowns in family relationships have forced or persuaded them to go as soon as they were able. The weakening of the family unit is a contributing factor and no one has assessed the impact of multiple divorces on the stability of young people.

Ideally young people should be able to make a gradual transition from a supportive family environment to independent living. Yet as the *Young Homelessness Group** suggests in its report *Moving On, Moving In*, 'there has been a failure to recognise the importance of leaving home as a natural event in the lives of young people, or to identify those skills, information and resources necessary to help them prepare for the process'.

Society has traditionally been unsympathetic to young people who leave home on impulse and there has been little commitment to meet their needs.

The explanation lies in part in the fact that British society is inconsistent in its attitudes towards young people. On the one hand they are encouraged to show initiative, to seek opportunities away from home and set off in search of work. On the other, they are criticised if they move and find themselves homeless, being considered feckless, work-shy and abusers of the social security system.

Several factors have played a part in conditioning public attitudes:

1 In 1975, the film 'Johnny Go Home' first caused a public outcry and put the issue of homelessness in the headlines for several months. Some of the voluntary projects consulted in this study owe their existence to the impact which that film made. But media attention is short-lived. Projects cannot survive on short-term interest. They require long-term commitment and funding if they are to contribute toward solving the housing needs of young people.

2 Disquiet and anger are expressed following criminal trials such as that of Dennis Nilson who persuaded homeless young men to go back to his house, where they were murdered. The Dennis Nilson case raised questions among parents, politicians and youth workers about how and why it happened and what could be done. There was little

---

* The Young Homelessness Group has tried to change attitudes by publicising the issue of homelessness in the wider context of young people's housing needs. Jointly funded by the Housing Campaign for Single Homeless People (CHAR) and Shelter (the National Campaign for the Homeless) it is a broad coalition of national housing and youth organisations which promotes better provision for young people in all sectors of the housing market.

9

long-term benefit, however, from the questions asked in Parliament and government attitudes towards young people have hardened.

3 Recently the DHSS Board and Lodging Regulations have actually legislated against young people by reducing the amount of benefit to which they were entitled and limiting the time over which it could be paid. A thoroughly distorted and exaggerated picture was painted of young people deliberately abusing the benefit system and living at public expense on the 'Costa del Dole'. This is symptomatic of central government's response which aims to make financial savings without considering the wider policy implications.

4 The task of raising children, providing them with food and shelter, ensuring they develop their potential as citizens, is the responsibility of parents. When the family unit breaks down, however, British society makes only minimal provision for the physical, emotional, and financial means of those young people who are above the school-leaving age.

5 Politicians and economists have advised young people to seek opportunities beyond their immediate environment, to 'get on their bikes' and look for work without any serious appraisal of the situation they face if they do just that. It is irresponsible and unrealistic for most young people and has been recognised as such by many youngsters.

Increasingly, young people are being portrayed as abusers or abused in an environment which they feel neither understands nor is able to respond to their needs: a society in which homelessness and unemployment are increasing among the young.

Inconsistency in the public's attitude to homelessness conditions the policy makers' response. A public outcry, fanned by the media, may generate some government action. But there is no clear strategy to meet the needs of homeless youth.

Those with the power to ease the plight of the young without a roof fail to face up to the problem. Public policy hides behind the stereotypes of homeless youngsters thought to be 'deviant' or responsible for their own fate. In the absence of an accurate assessment, stereotypes are considered to be self-evident truths.

Manchester City Council is untypical of housing authorities in recognising this. In its 'Hostel Replacement Programme' it points out that 'Far too often society blames the victims. People are homeless *not* because *they* have problems but because there is a housing problem – a desperate shortage of suitable housing, including care and support for those who need it. ... There is no statutory responsibility for single people who have nowhere to live. That is why nobody knows how many people are homeless.'

The Lack of Data

The issue of young people's homelessness remains unrecognised because it is unquantified. There are no accurate data. The evidence which exists is largely anecdotal and incomplete. On 26 October 1984 in answer to a Parliamentary question from Mr Alfred Morris MP, as to what information he had regarding the number of homeless adolescents in London and other major conurbations, Sir George Young for the Department of the Environment replied, 'This information is not available'. The Department of the Environment requires only basic data on homelessness from local authorities. Information includes neither the age nor family size of homeless people. The DHSS is equally remiss in not being able to supply comprehensive information about the number of young people who are homeless or living in hostels or other temporary accommodation.

Shelter (the National Campaign for the Homeless), in a forthcoming report,* has made the most detailed analysis of the evidence to date by surveying all local authority housing departments in England, Scotland and Wales, to establish how many homeless young people have applied for rehousing since the Housing (Homeless Persons) Act 1977. One in three of those who responded were unable to provide any statistical information. The agencies visited in the course of this study, however, confirm that homelessness among young people is rising rapidly.

---

* *Make Room for Youth*, to be published in Spring 1987.

An Increase in Homelessness

Between July and September 1985 the *Piccadilly Advice Centre* (PAC) in London dealt with 5,723 enquiries, an increase of 25 per cent on 1984. Of these 83 per cent related to accommodation, employment or financial matters. The most significant increase was in the number of enquiries about temporary accommodation which totalled 1,283 in a quarter, an increase of 52 per cent on the previous year.

The Centrepoint night shelter in Soho took in 2,159 homeless young people in 1984. Whereas it never used to turn people away, now it finds itself obliged to do so regularly. Faced with a demand far in excess of the number of beds, it was forced to reduce the age range for which it catered from 16–25 to 16–19 and still it is over-subscribed. Shades in Manchester sees an average of 45 people a month, 37 of whom are homeless. A GLC report claimed that the number of homeless people dealt with by London local authorities had multiplied sevenfold from 3,700 to 26,115 in 15 years.

No one knows how many people sleep rough in British streets. Workers at Centrepoint guess there are hundreds in London alone. A GLC survey 'Sleeping Out', in a limited area of London around the Embankment, Waterloo and the Temple found 3 per cent were teenagers and a further 20 per cent in their twenties. The latter group had almost doubled in size since a survey in 1965.

The reasons were made clear in the recent *Inquiry into British Housing* chaired by HRH the Duke of Edinburgh and published in July 1985. It stated: 'Very real housing problems are being experienced by many people with low and limited income. ... Most prominent among these is London which is now witnessing a serious increase in those who are statutorily homeless, those occupying bed-and-breakfast and emergency accommodation, and the numbers of single homeless people. ... In a number of areas there are simply not enough homes available.'

The Changing Nature of Homelessness

Homelessness arises from the general shortage of accommodation in towns, villages and cities, from the lack of appropriate, affordable accommodation and the failure of society to recognise the needs and desires of the present generation of youngsters for a place of their own.

The *Scottish Council for Single Homeless* in its report *Think Single*, published in 1981, assessed the accommodation experiences, needs and preferences of single people in Scotland. 56.9 per cent of those aged 16–19 were living at home. More than half of those who lived independently were in privately rented accommodation, 13 per cent lived in hostels, 13 per cent in lodgings and slightly fewer in local authority and owner-occupied dwellings. When questioned, the research showed that young people of 16–24 both preferred and relied on private, rented accommodation for their first move away from home. Yet this is the area of the housing market which has shrunk dramatically in recent years.

The Piccadilly Advice Centre reports that in the 1980s young people, recognising the difficulties of getting accommodation, have changed their attitude to moving away from home. In the 1960s young people were attracted to life in London, but equally they recognised the work opportunities London offered. Later, active encouragement was given to those in depressed areas to move to the South East in search of jobs. By the late 1970s getting established in London was not nearly so easy and many new arrivals were forced into the 'single homeless trap', in which someone without a job or money cannot secure accommodation and therefore cannot claim Supplementary Benefit.

The Salvation Army now see only four or five young people a night on their *Midnight Patrol* around London's St Pancras, Kings Cross, Euston and Paddington railway stations. While some of those who arrive in London are naive about what faces them, there is not the flood of young people to the capital that occurred in the happy-go-lucky days of the 1960s.

All housing agencies in London record a significant increase in requests for housing from homeless youngsters from the London boroughs; over 40 per cent of new callers each year at the *Alone in London* advice service come from the capital. In other cities, the main users of voluntary services, hostels and other projects are also from the city itself and adjacent areas. Seventy-six per cent of Shades users are from

Manchester and the North West and, of those, 58 per cent come from within the city. Eighty-eight per cent of residents at *Stopover*'s houses come from Edinburgh and adjacent areas. Of these, 120 previously lived at home, 54 with relatives, 60 with friends, 56 in bed-and-breakfast accommodation and 59 were sleeping rough in 1983/4.

Even those who come from areas near the city may not be able to gain access to local authority provision and this is where the role of voluntary agencies in plugging the gap and providing emergency cover is vital. *Blue Triangle*, a girls' hostel in Glasgow, had two girls resident from Bearsden, just six miles outside the city limits, for whom no provision was available other than a hostel in the city.

A probation officer in Wigan complained that the lack of local hostels obliged them to send young people into Manchester and considered this wholly unsatisfactory for 'local kids' needing emergency accommodation. The fact remains that there is no local authority responsibility for people from outside the area who have no connection with the city. Even where, as in Glasgow, the local authority houses 16- and 17-year-olds, those from outside are sent home with a DHSS travel warrant. The need for emergency accommodation to meet such situations has resulted in a new hostel initiative managed by the *Glasgow Council for the Single Homeless* (GCSH), which it is hoped will be operational during 1987.

Evidence of young people on the streets can be found in smaller towns such as Wigan, university and tourist towns such as Cambridge and new towns such as Livingston in Scotland. To some extent their situation is worse than that in the cities for there is little or no provision for them. When young people migrate from place to place it is often not from choice but because they feel they have no alternative in the area in which they grew up and in which, on the whole, they would prefer to stay.

Migration on a large scale does not appear to be a serious problem but there are no statistics. Agencies are concerned that a disproportionate number come to London and Manchester from Scotland and Ireland. Attempts have been made to discourage them, for example by the 'London

Calling'* exhibition held in Glasgow, but devised by PAC, which showed some of the pitfalls of moving south and the less attractive features of London. Three-quarters of those interviewed at the exhibition were definitely put off going to London as a result of it. Only 20 per cent still thought London offered them an opportunity. Preventive work is also being done in schools in Scotland; and the need for emergency accommodation for young people in Scotland has now been recognised and is being made available gradually. For those who do come to London, however, it is often a lonely and isolated trek in and out of bed-and-breakfast establishments.

---

* See Strathclyde Education Department report 'When I'm sixteen ... I'm leaving', a report on the survey carried out in connection with the 'London Calling' exhibition, 17–23 January 1983.

3
A PROFILE OF
HOMELESS YOUTH

Who Are Affected by Homelessness?

Contrary to popular belief, a young person may find himself
or herself homeless for a variety of reasons. The stereotypes
of homeless people as 'vagrants, dossers, feckless and inadequate' imply that individuals are responsible for their lack
of housing. PAC's experience shows that the youngsters who
come to the kiosk are ordinary people in circumstances
in which anyone could find themselves. The vast majority
of people they see are able, with assistance, to explain
their needs. And what they need is decent affordable
accommodation.

There is a difference, however, between identifying an
immediate need, such as a roof for tonight or for this week,
and obtaining a long-term solution, e.g. a bed-sit, tenancy,
shared accommodation or hostel place.

Young people seeking accommodation are not necessarily
surrounded by problems. Many are able to plan their move
from the family home and are helped to make that move
successful. Others, from stable backgrounds, may find themselves temporarily homeless and use the facilities offered by
the voluntary sector as a stop-gap. As the Blue Triangle hostel
warden said, 'We see girls from all walks of life – from stable
families and those whose relationships have broken down ...
it is not just "poor kids" any more'. There is no longer
any necessary connection between personal inadequacy
and homelessness, although those with a secure family
background may be less likely to find themselves destitute,

16

because they have an option (however undesirable to them) of ultimately returning to the family home. There is a difference between the needs and the ability to cope of those who have chosen to leave home, and of those who have been forced to leave and are homeless, destitute and demoralised.

Agencies providing drop-in facilities, counselling services and hostel accommodation, appreciate that some youngsters have particular needs and face a range of difficulties in retaining accommodation once they find it. Nearly all the residents at the Stopover hostel in Edinburgh arrive with some form of family breakdown behind them. 'The most common pattern is for young people to arrive fresh from a family crisis or to have moved from home into the bed-and-breakfast scene and then after further damaging experiences, to come to Stopover.' Seventy per cent of Stopover residents had lost a parent through divorce or death. Statistics from The Hyce, an emergency house run by the *Bridges Youth Project* in Hatfield, showed that, in nine out of eleven months of 1985, more than 70 per cent of residents were homeless as a result of a breakdown in the relationship with their parents or family. A Greater London Council (GLC) Survey in 1984 showed that one quarter of the 16–24 year-olds living in London hostels had left their last address as a result of a dispute with parents or partners. The Salvation Army's *259 Project*, which offers long-stay supported accommodation, reported that 90 per cent came from broken homes, whilst 63 per cent at the Children's Society's *Central London Teenage Project* suffered similarly. As Graeme Brown, the project leader, said, 'Our assumption is that young people do not run away if they are happy'.

The National Association for the Care and Resettlement of Offenders (NACRO) has drawn attention to the relationship between bad housing, homelessness and involvement in criminal activity. Particularly in London, the failure of DHSS payments to meet accommodation charges encourages young people into petty crime to raise the cash for a roof over their heads and food to eat.

Young People Who Have Been in Care

One of the most disturbing trends among the young homeless is the disproportionate number who come from local authority care. All projects highlighted this particular problem, which has been fully described in the Scottish Council for Single Homeless report *Where Am I Going to Stay?*

First Key, a national organisation set up to help young people leaving care, found that 7,000 youngsters under the age of 19 were homeless on leaving, or shortly after leaving, care. Twenty-two per cent of applicants to Stopover in Edinburgh in its first year and 13 per cent of applicants to Glasgow's homeless person's team had also come from residential care. These figures are significantly above the 5 per cent of the total population who have been in residential care.

The SCSH report is a catalogue of insufficient consultation, inadequate preparation of young people for independent living, lack of help and support after they leave, and a childhood characterised by instability, which repeats itself when the young people leave their residential home. Shelter even found young people sleeping in the grounds of a residential home in order to keep in touch with their friends. Almost all also faced unemployment, since they lacked basic educational qualifications and so had difficulty in maintaining a tenancy and managing on their limited income.

Some project workers expressed concern that the closure of residential homes had been carried out without proper planning, and that young people who left residential care in such circumstances were given no support when they tried to establish themselves in a tenancy.*

One project considered that social work teams placed adolescents low on their list of priorities and that increasing case loads reduced the time the team could spend on each problem. There was also concern that the substitution of foster homes for residential establishments was increasing the instability of some young people. Glasgow's single person's team were concerned at the high rate of foster care failures. This was aggravated by the falling status of children's homes which encouraged placements with foster families. Where adolescents proved difficult to control, it was claimed that foster parents 'threw them out' when they reached 18 since the foster parent received no further payment and had no further legal obligation. This requires further investigation.

---

* See Chapter 9 'The Role of the Statutory Sector'.

In general, the SCSH report confirms and extends the findings of a study for the National Association of Young People in Care (NAYPIC) which followed up all young people leaving care in Avon and Wakefield over a three-year period from 1982.

A number of national children's associations were running projects which offered 'independence training' for young people from residential homes. These ranged from supported accommodation with shared rooms and residential staff, to independent flats or bed-sits with limited social work support. The effectiveness of such projects remains to be tested. It was suggested that, in Scotland, great pride was taken in them, but that within 18 months ex-residents of independence projects often found themselves in Stopover.

Minority Groups

Projects in London aim to provide equally for black and white young people. The only black project visited commented that black youngsters were leaving home earlier than in the past, although the reasons had not been investigated. The information collected about the effect of homelessness on black and Asian youth is wholly inadequate. Few of the agencies visited referred to their needs and *UJIMA*, a housing association for Afro-Caribbean youth, was the only specifically black project mentioned.

A GLC report, referred to by Shelter, spells out the problems facing young black people who need to find a home of their own. 'Although much attention has been focused on the racial discrimination experienced by black people in seeking access to rented housing, most documented evidence does not consider the plight of those who perhaps face the greatest difficulties in gaining access to decent housing.' Shelter comments that black, and other ethnic minority, youth face all the problems arising from the lack of accommodation, with the additional barriers of racial discrimination. 'They often do not have access to voluntary groups and agencies which understand their specific problems and which can provide advice or referral and nomination to temporary or permanent housing with a housing association, co-op or borough council. The problems are particularly severe for young homeless girls and women.'

There is concern among London agencies about the extent of racism, both implicit and explicit, in the housing management policies of voluntary and statutory agencies, and discussions are being held to find ways of overcoming it. Racial discrimination, according to Shelter, manifests itself in many ways, continually blocking the housing opportunities for black youngsters. Housing advice agencies are often not readily accessible to black youth, and may have discriminatory referral or nomination procedures. Housing association allocation policies may also discriminate, while some private landlords compound racial discrimination with a refusal to house the unemployed, which makes it more difficult for black youth to secure affordable accommodation than white youngsters. Bed-and-breakfast establishments are also accused of having racist attitudes. So black single homeless people find themselves in a worse position than their white counterparts, who are themselves disadvantaged.

The indications are that homelessness among young black people will continue to rise, and the lack of black housing workers in the field exacerbates their problems. The information obtained from UJIMA gives some idea of the scale of the problem.

UJIMA was formed in 1977 by a group of black housing workers who were concerned by the problems of housing and homelessness among young single people of ethnic minority origin. The Association has grown rapidly during the past four years and, in addition to self-contained housing, has hostels and bedsits all over London. In September 1985 they managed 219 short-life properties, 16 hostels and group homes, and a substantial number of units are in the process of being built. As a result of its initial success, the Association has begun to move away from short-life housing and to provide good quality, permanent, purpose-built accommodation.

The Association caters for young people aged 17–30 who need housing. They find that under-17s have difficulty maintaining their tenancies and they will not house those for whom there is a local authority responsibility, e.g. pregnant girls or those with mental or physical disabilities. This has proved to be a bone of contention with the Probation Service.

Young people may be referred by Housing Advice Centres and other agencies, although 50 per cent refer themselves. The workers aim to place those who are eligible into mainstream housing. Most come from the London area and 31 per cent of those housed are unemployed. The accommodation available is substantially over-subscribed. In Lewisham for example, there were 326 people on a waiting list and only two properties in the pipeline. In July 1985 there were 1,863 men and 1,475 women awaiting housing, of whom 62.6 per cent were aged 18–24. 69 per cent were of West Indian origin, but mostly UK-born. 21 per cent were living with parents, 56 per cent with friends temporarily.

The *Short Stay Young Homeless Project*'s hostel at Bina Gardens, which caters for equal proportions of black and white youth, is over-subscribed, as are the *Longstop Project*'s flats and bed-sits in Lewisham. Much more attention needs to be given to the needs of black youth for housing and to the racist attitudes from which they suffer.

Another area which is particularly under-researched is the needs of ethnic women. A project in Manchester for Asian women is currently seeking hostel funding because of concern about Asian girls running away from family conflict, arranged marriages and traditional pressures.

New Horizon Youth Centre was so concerned at its failure to attract young women and black people that it reconsidered its programmes and has tried to have one day a week specifically for women, and organises certain activities for women only.

Few projects commented on the housing requirements of homosexual and lesbian groups, although in London there are some housing associations which cater specifically for them. Shades caters for a significant number of homosexuals but has found that they want to be offered mainstream provision and not placed together in ghettos.

Age of Homeless Young People

Once again, inadequate data make any assessment difficult. The ages recorded depend largely on the age limits set by the projects themselves and by the agencies working with homeless young people. 56.5 per cent of Stopover's residents from 1981/4 were aged 16 and 17. At Bridges the average age was between 18 and 19 but under-16 referrals were also received. Sixty-five per cent of men visiting Shades are between 16 and 20.

Age is particularly relevant in discussing youth homelessness because of the legal implications. Young people can legally leave home at the age of 16 without parental consent and can legally marry. Yet few local authorities feel able or willing to grant tenancies before the age of 18. In Glasgow and Manchester, where the city councils give priority to housing young people under 18, Single Person's Officers were not conscious of age being relevant to housing problems. Neither authority was able to monitor its placements, however, to see whether the policy was successful and whether young people had needs which were not met within orthodox housing management policies.

In London, in particular, there is concern among a number of agencies at the increasing evidence of teenage runaways aged under 16. A random survey of 387 young people viewing the touring exhibition entitled 'London Calling' in Glasgow in January 1983 showed that 134 (87 males and 47 females) had run away from home at some time. This was 34.6 per cent of those interviewed. More than half of those who had run away had stayed away for more than a day and a night. 72.3 per cent gave problems within the home as their main reason for running away. PAC considered that the problem was exaggerated and no one is claiming that the numbers are very large. But a need has been clearly demonstrated and the concern of the London agencies led to the establishment of the Central London Teenage Project.

The Salvation Army and Bridges commented on the inadequacies of the legal system, which requires under-16s to be returned to their home, or to the Social Services Department in their home area, if they are subject to a Care Order. This merely treated the symptom, they felt. It did nothing to explain why the person had run away and made them wonder whether sending him/her home would result in other than a recurrence of the problems which had caused him or her to run away in the first place.

Critics of 'runaway' programmes suggest that, by providing a safe house, organisations are removing parental authority and encouraging youngsters to leave home. All projects concerned with teenagers deny that allegation and the evidence confirms their position.

The Short Stay Young Homeless Project, Bridges and the Teenage Project try to find out about the home relationship in order to establish whether a resident can go home and if a reconciliation is possible. In an article in *Scottish Child*, Autumn 1985, John Cran, project worker at the Monklands Refuge for 14–17-year-olds, comments: 'Reconciliation is the real business of the Refuge and reconciliation works. In the last 10 months we have had 110 referrals and only 10 of those have left home for any length of time.' While young people were not unduly pressured (and always had the freedom to walk out on the projects) the choices facing them were spelt out candidly, and for teenagers under 16 those choices were extremely limited. Legally, an under-16 year-old cannot be offered permanent employment, cannot claim Supplementary Benefit, or have access to anything other than temporary accommodation. In the city they would be forced into illegal activities almost immediately. Experience at the Teenage Project shows that, on average, people stay only four days while research is done into their backgrounds. Running away is a *cri de cœur* and what appears necessary is a breathing space, which safe houses, sensitively run, can provide. The teenagers may be able to return home on their own terms and try to re-establish family relationships.

Gender of the Homeless

The data obtained on the sex of homeless people was inconclusive. Shelter estimates that women comprise 20 per cent of homeless young people but this was not borne out by the project data. Centrepoint's night shelter saw 1,600 males and 500 females in 1984, while the figures for the Stopover hostel in Edinburgh were 266 and 230 respectively. In July 1985, 338 men and 203 women called at the Piccadilly Advice Centre, while in its first few months of operation the Teenage Project catered for 52 per cent boys and 48 per cent girls. Women were also in the minority at Shades (65 per cent to 35 per cent) and at the Cambridge 'drop-in' bus run by the *Cyrenians*.

Some workers thought that there were fewer homeless women because they were more likely to stay with friends, and talk through their problems. Shades considered that they remained within the 'hidden homeless' because they were more likely to put up with circumstances which men would not tolerate. Since homelessness is always measured at the

24

point of provision and there is little provision for women, their needs, according to Shades, 'remain trapped in a circle of invisibility'.

Projects, which like the Short Stay Young Homeless Project at Bina Gardens in London have an equal-opportunities policy, do not have problems in filling their beds. The Hyce, run by Bridges, also provides for equal numbers of men and women.

Two day centres stress that the lack of women using their facilities is because they are not sufficiently attractive to women. Shades saw a need 'to curtail and control the male atmosphere which sometimes prevails' so that young women feel welcome. Their outreach work will be redirected to places which young women use. The New Horizon Youth Centre was so concerned at its failure to attract young women and black people that it is reconsidering its programme and intends to have one day a week specifically for women, when there will be an all-women team working to counteract an otherwise male-dominated centre.

4
THE RESPONSE OF THE VOLUNTARY SECTOR TO HOUSING NEED

Most of the voluntary organisations working with homeless youth see their role, at least in part, as helping the young person identify his/her housing options. Almost inevitably there has to be a compromise between the desires and the reality. But, once a decision has been reached, front-line agencies such as Alone in London, Piccadilly Advice Centre or housing aid centres will assist the young person in his search for a roof. The solution may be short-term: finding a crash pad or night shelter, or bed-and-breakfast for a day or two; or securing a place in a short-stay hostel where a person's needs can be more clearly established over a period of time. Or it may be finding longer-term provision in a long-stay hostel, as a tenant with a housing association, or in some cases with a local authority or other public agency.

Night Shelters and Emergency Accommodation

Of approximately 15 emergency night shelters in London only one, Centrepoint, Soho, caters specifically for young people. Standards vary and even those with the lowest standards are often full. Centrepoint in 1983 received 10,493 requests for admission and was able to provide shelter for 2,076. It averages 90 per cent occupancy over the year. Bina Gardens was able to accommodate only half of those referred to it.

In 1983 *Emergency*, a London-based campaign, studied six central London night shelters which accepted young people. Its report concluded that provision was 'characterised by

archaic buildings, poor standards, myriad rules and regulations and under-staffing'. The shelters surveyed included two
DHSS Resettlement Units and four voluntary hostels. The
report revealed that the premises were old, with attendant
problems of disrepair, and were being put to a use for which
they were not designed. They included churches, schools,
hospitals and crypts.

There is a heavy dependence on volunteers in all the voluntary sector projects. Because of the institutional nature of
night shelters, rules and regulations abound. Once in, residents are often not allowed to go out until the following
morning. The projects vary in their policies towards friends
and visitors. At Centrepoint, 32 young people sleep in bunks
in two small rooms in a crypt. It has recently been refurbished
and is clean, but there is no privacy and residents have to
be out by 8 a.m. to roam the streets in search of a better
alternative.

While most shelters offer advice on accommodation, few
of their residents were found permanent accommodation.
Centrepoint has developed follow-on accommodation
specifically for young people at Bina Gardens, which is a
short-stay house; a long-stay hostel in Hammersmith and 30
bed-sits are also available. The workers at Centrepoint believe emergency shelters should not have to exist in their
present form. It is generally accepted that the closure of night
shelters in cities is a matter for celebration, so appalling are
the standards with an atmosphere more representative of the
19th than the 20th century.

The voluntary sector cannot escape criticism for continuing to offer an inappropriate response. But voluntary agencies find themselves locked into an impossible situation. In
the West End of London, for example, property is both
expensive and difficult to obtain. They do not have the funds
to provide the quality of accommodation that they feel young
people deserve. Some large organisations are faced with
modernising large, outdated and inappropriate buildings.
The voluntary sector does not have the resources to do this.
While theirs may be an insufficient response, it is preferable
to nothing – and if they were to withdraw, they fear that
would be the result. To achieve the improvements they wish
to see, attitudes must change dramatically and there must be

greater support for the voluntary agencies from both central and local government.

Society responds slowly to changes in demand. Provision of services will always lag behind the need. Many night shelters have closed in recent years and too few bed spaces have been found to replace them. The closure of DHSS resettlement units such as Camberwell put pressure on London agencies, since provision in the capital is totally inadequate. There is also considerable pressure on voluntary agencies in the rest of Britain, although the numbers are fewer.

Voluntary agencies are no longer able to offer free beds for those who are destitute. The numbers wanting accommodation are too high and voluntary agencies depend on the revenue from letting accommodation, as well as on charitable donations, to meet their overheads. An exception to this is the provision for up to three young people a night who are stranded at Euston, Paddington, St Pancras or King's Cross station and who may be offered shelter by the Midnight Patrol. The Salvation Army have an arrangement with Camden Council and the DHSS so that they are reimbursed for any homeless person housed overnight through the Midnight Patrol.

Bed-and-breakfast hotels have, from lack of alternatives, become the main source of emergency provision. Millions of pounds of public money are paid every year to landlords who provide overcrowded, inadequate and insecure accommodation. Accommodation for which Supplementary Benefit payments are made should be subject to inspection and perhaps licences should be issued. Shades operates a black list of bed-and-breakfast hotels felt to be particularly bad and some local authorities are doing this too.

Inner and outer London boroughs did not on the whole consider it part of their responsibility to provide emergency accommodation specifically for young people, although some make grants to voluntary organisations to do so. Lack of provision in the boroughs means that emergency care tends to be concentrated in the city centre and not where it is most needed – in the locality where young people are homeless.

Projects agree on the need for emergency provision for young people as a safety net and an entry point to more satisfactory provision. Outside London, the numbers of beds required are not excessive. Despite lack of local authority emergency accommodation in Manchester, Shades' overnight crash pad arrangement has taken an average of only nine people each night. It offers an interesting approach, using spare accommodation in people's homes, usually members of Shades, for up to three nights. It depends, however, on goodwill and is by definition temporary. Stopover in Edinburgh accommodates up to 12. Bridges offers 6–8 beds. While there is a crucial need for emergency access so that young people do not have to sleep rough, many small-scale local initiatives would be more appropriate than large shelters. They are inevitably less institutionalised and more akin to a home. Manchester City Council is evolving a scheme using four properties in the north, south and east of the city, and in Wythenshawe, for direct access emergency provision. There will also be a direct access short-stay hostel in the city centre.

Voluntary agencies favour the development of small direct access hostels such as are being developed in Glasgow and Livingston. They must be of high quality, adequately staffed, with good working conditions. Open at all times, they should not have limits on the length of stay. Young people can then be given time in a supportive environment to assess their needs and be assisted in finding a longer-term solution. It should be a local solution and not require or encourage them to move to city centres. One organisation particularly opposed the notion of young people being given an emergency bed through the dark hours and then being despatched to day centres 'to be kept occupied' and off the streets.

A homely, caring environment, properly staffed and serviced should be available. The strategy put forward by the *Housing Campaign for Single Homeless People* (CHAR) and endorsed in general by a number of agencies, is that emergency accommodation should be provided as part of a range of housing to meet the needs of young people. CHAR considers that the provision should be managed by local housing authorities but others would be satisfied with a partnership approach. Where provided, it should:

● Provide good standard accommodation with single rooms.

● Have a maximum of 30 bed spaces.

● Be adequately staffed, with good working conditions, and open to residents at all times.

- Have no limits on length of stay.
- Have links with a range of other accommodation and services.

Substandard provision should be phased out as soon as appropriate arrangements can be made.

Hostels

Well-run, adequately resourced hostels have an advantage over night shelters because they are more comfortable, offer more privacy in single or shared rooms than the dormitories of old and, where a homely atmosphere is fostered, they can offer joint activities for residents. Hostel developments have been the most rapid area of growth in provision for young people in recent years. Voluntary organisations have encouraged, supported and actively participated in their establishment. Partnership schemes with local authorities and housing associations have evolved and some of these initiatives are of a very high standard.

Work undertaken by the Scottish Council for Single Homeless shows considerable support for hostels as long as they are clear about their aims, provide a high standard of accommodation and are adequately staffed. There is now a strategy for developing this provision in Scotland and to assist those trying to do the same elsewhere. SCSH has produced an excellent book on *Hostel Funding*.

There are differences of view between agencies on hostel provision – differences based on political assessments of what type of provision is appropriate for young people and who should provide it, as well as on whether the voluntary sector should plug gaps which some think should be filled by the statutory sector.

A few projects feel that providing hostels is not the answer to young people's housing needs. 'Hostels provide only band-aid ... plastering over the cracks ... they can only be a temporary solution. If you take on a commitment to a young person you can't stop part way through.' Two projects do not liaise with hostels at all but seek long-term solutions. New Horizon Youth Centre places young people straight into flats through the Housing Services Agency.

Large city-centre hostels, which traditionally catered for older institutional men with alcohol or psychiatric problems, are not appropriate for young people. Manchester City Council is in the process of implementing its strategy of closing the big old hostels on which vast sums of money would need to be spent. It is also assisting voluntary organisations in running down their outdated provision. A night shelter has already closed. A survey of residents of all ages in the hostels showed that 85 per cent wanted to live in independent accommodation; 50 per cent wanted it furnished. None wished to live in a big hostel. The size of the programme they have taken on, however, has delayed its implementation. The organisers of the 259 Project for young men based in a Salvation Army men's hostel, recognise that the location is not ideal and are looking for a better one, but they say that it offers a means of social control, and that young people take pride that their future will be better than those who seek refuge in the hostel.

Two projects considered that, while such institutional hostels provide a cheap bed, a considerable number of young people come away from them with more problems than they had in the beginning. No support services are available in those hostels and the needs of residents are not questioned.

In one case the DHSS had wanted the voluntary sector to take on the management of a resettlement unit but this had been resisted, for there was no guarantee of funding from the Government to meet the running costs. With a commitment that funds would be provided, the voluntary organisations in London would have been willing to consider taking the unit under their wing.

Some hostels, e.g. Stopover, Manchester and Blue Triangle, have developed to meet particular needs such as provision for homeless young women. These have varying levels of official support.

The main distinctions which appeared in this survey were between long-stay and short-stay hostels, and between those which were direct-access (e.g. Stopover, Edinburgh, Blue Triangle) and those which mainly took referrals through local social services departments. Many of the latter had been developed by child-care agencies in response to the need for independence-training and therefore a higher level of support than other hostels.

Since the private rented sector has dried up almost totally – except for those who can provide sound references, a substantial deposit or payment in advance and sometimes a guarantor – the demand for hostel places is too big to be met. Bina Gardens receives 30–35 referrals per week for 5–6 places. Short-stay hostels, such as Stopover in Manchester (three weeks), Stopover, Edinburgh (eight weeks) and Bina Gardens (four weeks) have the aim of providing short-term accommodation while a proper assessment of needs is carried out and firm arrangements can be made for the young person to move on. Staff try to establish quickly the resident's medium- and long-term housing needs, and then seek a place where those needs can be met. This is a necessary, but some consider unsatisfactory, part of total provision. Unsatisfactory, because it reinforces the temporary nature of provision for young people and does not necessarily resolve their problems.

For some young people, who are not sure what their needs are and whether they wish to settle in the area, short-stay hostels provide a temporary breathing space which is valuable and saves resources being wasted on finding a permanent solution which may not be appropriate. All the hostels give assistance in finding accommodation. There are different approaches. Some do it on behalf of the young person, while others assist him or her to make the arrangements. Increasingly, short-stay hostels are being required to extend the length of stay because no satisfactory longer-term places can be found.

Success in placing people depends entirely on local provision. Bina Gardens now often finds itself unable to place residents in follow-on accommodation and has had to lengthen the stay from four to six weeks. Blue Triangle has extended provision from three to nine months. Manchester Stopover, however, finds it possible to provide accommodation within the time limit and this ranges from a local authority flat to a return to bed-and-breakfast or another hostel. It succeeds because staff have very good links with a housing authority which has accepted responsibility for housing single homeless people and is developing its policy for the under-18s.

Level of support

Most short-stay hostels themselves question how much support they can give. By and large, emphasis is on making the residents feel welcome and at ease, identifying their needs and helping in a practical way to cope with the details of, and personnel involved in, the welfare benefits and unemployment offices. Some, such as Bina Gardens, recognise that they are not staffed to give more than limited counselling or simple referrals.

Those set up to provide 'emergency help' are not able to be flexible and extend the length of stay, because of excessive demand, the aim of encouraging a high turnover, and the lack of staff support to meet the longer-term needs of many young people. Short-stay hostels recommend referral to appropriate agencies and give support in, for instance, obtaining benefits or looking for work. They do not set out to provide emotional and psychological counselling to more than a superficial extent. Too many people return to them having failed to solve their fundamental problems and in need of recurrent support. Stopover, Edinburgh, candidly admits that 'Many young people arrive at Stopover requiring more support than we can possibly offer'. Pressure on bed spaces obliges short-stay hostels to be highly selective in the people they accept, often excluding those who require more than minimal support.

Run by the YWCA, the Blue Triangle tries to mix unemployed, homeless young girls with those who are working. It has not been successful. Girls with jobs became work-shy. They were disrupted by those who did not have commitments during the day and so turned night into day in the hostel, staying up late and causing disturbances, until those with employment were unable to continue their jobs. Now the hostel will take just three employed girls, each with a particularly stable background and strong personality, to stand up to those whose behaviour is disruptive. A further nine are referred from a range of agencies. These are often from disturbed backgrounds, involved in crime or prostitution and requiring substantial assistance.

Standards

High-quality accommodation is needed if young people are to be offered an acceptable solution to their housing and other needs. Some would choose to live in a hostel rather than in a more independent establishment and, for some young people, this is an appropriate form of accommodation for a period in their lives. There is a trend toward single rooms where facilities allow, and only a few projects still have three- or four-bedded rooms. Hostels which offer a high standard of accommodation find that the residents respect it and there are fewer problems of damage, graffiti and untidiness than those which are old, dilapidated and poorly furnished. When *Glengowan* hostel in Glasgow was refurbished in 1985, boys who had not had contact with parents for a year or two began to invite their families to visit as they were proud of their house.

Long-stay hostels provide a bridge for some young people between a children's home or supportive family environment and independent living. Most of the hostels visited were single-sex, provided extensive support and were in residential areas with shops and on bus routes. All the long-stay hostels visited took a substantial proportion of their referrals – the National Children's Home (NCH) exclusively – from social services. They usually had multiple deprivation and family breakdown to contend with. Some of their residents were seriously disturbed. Yet they had no more, sometimes fewer, staff than the short-stay projects.

Exclusions

All agencies are clear about exclusions. None of the residential projects visited, with the exception of *Kaleidoscope*, a multiple project including a hostel, youth club, residential and other services, would take young people with a history of drug abuse. Only Kaleidoscope and Blue Triangle took people with a dependence on alcohol. Project staff at the *Hungerford Drug Project* felt that the housing position facing their clients was desperate.

Forty per cent of the clients who approached the Hungerford Drug Project in 1983/4 were homeless or living in temporary or unsatisfactory accommodation (including bed-and-breakfast, hostels, squats and with friends). They understood the insistence of those running housing projects for young people that they remain within the law and ensure that drugs are not taken on their premises. However, the total exclusion of drug users from such projects made it extremely difficult to meet their housing needs. They also regretted the fact that many housing project staff closed their minds to the drug problem. They hoped that training could be arranged for housing workers so that they could both recognise those with a drug problem and know what could be done to help them both with their dependency and in housing. Some ex-users who had had therapy and/or rehabilitation could benefit from housing provided by voluntary organisations and it was felt that a few projects should be developed to respond to this need. Most remained in sub-standard bed-and-breakfast accommodation. Small hostels might, it was felt, lessen the dependence of homeless drug users on the West End networks.

It was generally felt that young people with such problems should be referred to agencies with staff qualified to deal with them. There are voluntary projects specifically for drug users in London and other cities but they were not studied as part of this project. According to the city council, there was no such provision in Glasgow.

Only the long-stay projects with a residential social work component are willing to consider young people with a history of violence or psychiatric problems. Blue Triangle, Glengowan boys' hostel and the National Children's Home *Elmstead Woods* independence project in Surrey successfully manage the people in their care but also maintain firm discipline and substantial, but friendly, control.

Evictions

Some projects also have policies on evictions. Few projects consider taking back anyone who was evicted but tolerance levels before evicting vary. Some evict immediately if rules are broken – such as violence towards another resident, damage to property or racism. Others have a warning system. In general, the projects founded on social work principles are more tolerant. They recognise that, for many of their residents, there is nowhere else to go. However, the projects are dependent on social services to maintain the level of their referrals and hence their income. Over-demand means that independent hostels can enforce the rules strictly.

Staffing

The ideal staffing level for a hostel is considered to be approximately eight staff to twelve residents to give reasonable 24-hour cover. With staff working a 35-hour week and taking into account time off and sickness, this number is necessary. Stopover, Edinburgh, feels that a high level of staff support is essential to help the residents assess their housing requirements, make sensible choices and apply for accommodation. Their tasks range from providing local newspapers which advertise accommodation and access to a telephone, to helping residents get an interview with the housing department; offering support at a meeting with the job centre; giving welfare rights advice and encouraging survival skills, such as cookery or budgeting. If the level of support for residents is to be improved or the service developed, the staff must of course be expanded.

The Central London Teenage Project requires nine staff, including an administrator, a researcher, a senior social worker, five professional workers and a CSV volunteer. None of the staff is resident but 24-hour cover is provided. Since referrals are taken throughout the night, the staff work on a shift system. They used the time between their appointment and the opening of the project for training, and have arranged locum cover so that, from time to time, staff can meet and evaluate the way the project is developing. This is invaluable in a new and innovative project.

Most voluntary projects fail to achieve this level of staffing because of inadequate funding. They showed evidence of under-staffing and commented that this limited their effectiveness. Hungerford, for example, in response to increased demand for advice and counselling had been forced to withdraw its street-based service. Having now been able to reinstate a detached worker, the benefit was immediate in re-establishing contacts and making new contacts with drug

37

users. Small projects, and those with insufficient funding to meet desired staffing levels, are vulnerable if an emergency arises, and they become dangerously dependent on a key worker, for direction, management and day-to-day support.

In *Bury*, Lancashire, managers of a short-stay semi-supportive hostel run in conjunction with North British Housing Association, had to make a decision to withdraw staff overnight in order to campaign and give sufficient support during the day. The residents responded well to the withdrawal of night cover and staff wondered whether their presence at night had fostered disquiet and friction. There were fewer problems after they withdrew.

Links between hostels and permanent accommodation

Ideally hostel projects should have close links with follow-on accommodation so that there is access to independent units when their residents are ready for it. In an attempt to over-come lack of this follow-on accommodation, several hostels and other projects have developed their own long-term provision, or joined with housing associations to gain access to permanent accommodation.

Bridges is evolving three stages from emergency and inten-sive provision, to a long-stay hostel, and then to independent flats and bed sits managed by the National Children's Home in conjunction with Bridges, the Voluntary Workers Trust, the County Council and the District Council. The aim is to enable people to move back and forth between the various stages with the added options of alternative hostels and land-ladies as their needs change. A community-based social worker co-ordinates these options. In Bury, the hostel set up a landlady scheme and attempts are also being made to acquire follow-on properties.

Shades links with a range of co-operative flats and short-life property through a housing association. In Scotland, Stopover's management committee manages two supported flats leased from the Fountainbridge Housing Association, as an experiment. It has shown that, with adequate preparation and initial support, young people can become acceptable tenants without the need for continuing support. The hostel is now trying to encourage housing associations to become more involved.

The West End agencies in London, and particularly Centrepoint, Soho, have developed their own follow-on facilities because of the lack of alternatives. Bina Gardens has an option on long-stay accommodation at its second project in Holloway Road, while the 259 Project has leased training flats from the Salvation Army and a local authority to use as a half-way stage to full independence. Such developments are particularly important in London because of the shortage of accommodation.

Follow-on provision has been developed because projects cannot function without it and want to be able to offer a permanent solution to their residents. Where local authorities do not provide access to housing for young single people, the voluntary sector is an essential provider.

Relations with the community

All the hostels are conscious of the need to keep a discreet profile in the local community. They do not wish to draw attention to the young people in the hostels, nor to create tension with neighbours. Most of the schemes maintain good relations, though Bina Gardens has had a few problems arising from visitors. Visiting is allowed in all the hostels, but the time allowed varies. Bina Gardens has had to restrict it severely because of pilfering and noise.

Relationships with local police are also variable. Bridges, being located in two police houses, finds the police supportive, particularly when dealing with teenage runaways. The Central London Teenage Project could not have functioned without the co-operation of the Metropolitan Police and B14 Missing Person's Division. Project staff contact the Bureau, with the knowledge of the young person, when a new resident arrives and has identified him/herself. In Glasgow, the police regularly return girls found soliciting to the Blue Triangle hostel. Longstop in Lewisham, however, are concerned about their bad relationship with the police. Project staff commented on racist attitudes and the failure of the police to come out when there was trouble.

Given the sensitive nature of the work, and the illegal

nature of many of the activities with which it comes into contact, the Hungerford project has a good working relation with local police, although occasionally problems arise. The project is located on a police training beat and cadets are sometimes insensitive in their approach, or cause problems through not knowing the project and its work. At street level there can be difficulties as the project is in a very heavily policed area of London. The police personnel change frequently and are consequently less likely to know the project workers.

Outreach and follow-up support

The most effective hostels find it insufficient for their contact support to end with longer-term housing. Stopover in Edinburgh and Manchester, Blue Triangle and Bridges have all found it desirable to maintain contact with young people in their new homes, and to help them to settle. Blue Triangle uses home-makers, who visit the girls every week in the beginning and then fortnightly until they become established. Girls are also encouraged to come back to the hostel for visits, so that they do not become isolated once they have their own accommodation. Follow-up is limited for it has to be done in the staff's free time. Fifty per cent of Stopover, Manchester's ex-residents come back to visit staff and friends, and extension work is now given priority. Glengowan has also come to an arrangement whereby a youth can come back and spend one night a week in the hostel after being rehoused to maintain contact and stability until he is established. The young men are encouraged to help decorate the flats obtained for residents and, once rehoused, to help each other if problems arise.

Stopover in Edinburgh provides support in resettling residents and in obtaining DHSS payments, dealing with officialdom and trying to get a job. It liaises with a youth link scheme which provides volunteer support for young people who have left care. This is run by Family Care, whose workers are willing to extend their service to ex-Stopover residents. Bridges also offers help in this way, and a befriending service for those in lodgings. Lack of staff means this side of the work is largely dependent on volunteer input.

Bridges and Blue Triangle also emphasised the importance of local community links so that their work would be valued and supported, financially and socially. Bridges runs a crèche, and offers access to daytime activities for non-residents and past residents. Blue Triangle offers a meeting room to a pensioners' group. Funds raised from hiring out facilities are used to improve the facilities for the girls so that they see a direct connection between their provision for others and their own gain. They recognise that it would not always be possible for such links to be established but are particularly keen to continue this involvement. In Bridges this has led to extensive mutual support for those who were new and those who, eight years after the project's formation, were now living a comparatively stable life.

Housing Associations

Housing associations* have played an important part in providing long-term housing for young people. They are non-profit bodies run by voluntary committees providing housing and hostel places at fair rents. In partnership with voluntary organisations, they have allowed innovative management techniques to be developed to give support to young people trying to obtain housing. They are good at helping young people to untangle the 'red tape' of public housing provision.

Housing associations offer furnished and unfurnished accommodation, shared and single tenancies. This is particularly valuable since it meets directly the needs expressed by young people. The SCSH report, *Think Single*, showed that 29 per cent of 16–29-year-olds want 'one-person' accommodation, yet only 7 per cent are able to get it.

Several projects offer examples of working in partnership with housing associations. Most act as managing agents for properties owned by housing associations. Longstop's ex-

---

* The National Federation of Housing Associations produces a comprehensive range of publications for those interested in setting up, or working with, a housing association, including a 'Housing Association Registration Information Pack'; 'Special Projects through Housing Associations' – a guide for a project group or voluntary organisation considering a partnership with a housing association to establish a special project; and a 'Guide for Housing Associations Working with Voluntary Organisations'.

perience is interesting in this context and is explained in detail below.

Longstop was set up as a pilot project to help identify the housing needs of young single homeless people in Lewisham, London and to develop appropriate management practice.

With the decline in rented accommodation in the borough, a Youth Aid Housing Group (Longstop's predecessor) took over a short-life property for conversion with the aim of providing medium-term accommodation for young people. From this, Longstop grew and now manages six housing association and one local authority house. Referrals come from within the Borough, mainly through two drop-in centres and a local hostel. Applicants are interviewed by the management workers and other residents before being accepted. There is an extensive system of support workers who visit the residents more than once a week to check how things are going, assist with DHSS claims, or other financial matters, and ensure rents do not get into arrears.

Residents are encouraged to hold house meetings and to sort out problems collectively. On average, they stay for 15 months, although the trend now is to stay longer because there are insufficient places for people to move on to. No waiting list is kept, but there is always a queue for each vacancy. Vacancies arise about twice a month and there are too few properties for people to move on from Longstop when they are ready. Other available permanent accommodation is in areas which are unsuitable, particularly for young single women.

People are evicted for rent arrears, violence, drug abuse and not taking part in the household. This is, however, a last resort and only two people were evicted last year. The strength lies in making the right placements in the first place and preventing the build-up of arrears by using the system of payment of rent direct. 64 per cent of residents who left in 1984/5 went on to permanent accommodation.

Problems do arise in the management of properties, particularly in a high density inner city area. Longstop residents have faced internal and external problems of security, so now all houses have an inter-com system.

The project operates an equal opportunities policy between men and women and between black and white residents. This has proved to be successful.

Management Policies
The first house showed that there was a limit to the number of people who could share successfully. Eight residents were found to be too many to prevent friction when there were insufficient bathroom and kitchen facilities. Communal living rooms were only used where there was a television and, since listening to music was a common pastime, lack of sound-proofing caused problems, both in the house and with neighbours.

The project has now evolved specialised housing designs. Caretakers live in and give the residents a sense of stability.

They reduce the day-to-day problems for management workers by dealing with some repairs and domestic issues. The worker can then interview all prospective residents and explain what is expected of them. Since 75 per cent of residents are unemployed, the worker also offers support and advice, especially in the area of welfare rights and housing benefits. While management workers collect the rents, they see their role as much more important than that of a rent collector. They are not able to take on anyone with drug or alcohol problems, a history of violence or other problems. There are two housing management workers, one development and finance worker, and an administrator.

Relations with other organisations are good. Longstop is highly respected and so feels it has influence with the borough council and with referral agencies. Agencies know the type of person who is likely to be placed by Longstop and so do not waste staff time with inappropriate referrals.

Funding comes from the GLC and Lewisham Borough Council. A Hostel Deficit Grant covers the cost of the workers, and rents, housing benefit and donations make up the rest.

The project has deliberately restricted its expansion since it is a pilot project and wants scope to experiment with different management styles. The future depends on government policies both centrally and locally. It is intended that Lewisham will take back the short-life properties and maintain the intensive management support. Whether they will be able to do that depends, it is felt, more on issues of funding than commitment to the project, which is high. The project could expand and take on the management of more properties, but this would require more workers and bigger offices. Staff would like to be able to offer a drop-in advice service for residents, encourage development of a newsletter and group activities. Time will tell whether these evolve.

Other projects with housing associations, such as Shades Community Action Project, have also found it helpful to employ caretakers on site to provide support if equipment breaks down or repairs are required to the property. Shades, like Longstop, did not involve caretakers in management, placing tenants or rent-collecting.

UJIMA employs resettlement workers to help residents settle in and offers assistance with any problems which arise. They feel that this is essential if a tenancy is to become established, and consider that tenants do not wish to be involved in management decisions. With 140 short-life properties, UJIMA is one of the most rapidly growing housing associations. Rapid growth has brought its own problems and they are able to offer no more than minimal support to tenants. So selection procedures are rigorous.

Since housing associations operate locally and are small compared with a local authority housing department, they are able to offer a highly personal service and meet their tenants regularly.

Co-ordinated Responses to Young People's Housing

Several of the projects in Surrey, London, Manchester and Hatfield are broadly based and incorporate several of the elements described in this chapter. Particularly in small towns, where the problems faced by homeless young people are substantial but the numbers are not excessive, there is much to be said for comprehensive projects or for networking between small-scale projects. In a city the size of Glasgow or London, it is not possible for one agency to provide a comprehensive response.

Examples are given in detail here of:

1 Bridges in Hatfield
2 West End Co-Ordinated Voluntary Service in London

They show first how a small project can develop to provide a comprehensive response to the problem of youth homelessness, and how a number of agencies work together to prevent duplication and make the most effective use of limited resources.

1 *Bridges* is a wide-ranging project offering a drop-in day centre, emergency accommodation in The Hyce, intensive counselling, practical, emotional and personal support, and an advice service for young people aged 16–30.

Set up in 1973 it aimed to 'work with young people on the fringes of society'. It operated on the premise that these young people were 'largely bankrupt of love and affection' and had often been rejected. The project aimed to encourage young people to believe in themselves, to bring about change so that they could live a healthier and, it is to be hoped, happier life.

Historically, Bridges was particularly involved with young-

44

sters suffering from addictions and ran a centre for them. They soon found that the users broke into the hall at night, as many were homeless and needed a safe place to sleep. So The Hyce was acquired to provide emergency accommodation. The project is now housed in two short-life properties. The premises are small, over-crowded and dilapidated. They are totally inadequate to meet the needs of the staff and users. But the inadequacies of the premises are more than compensated for by the people, the supportive, friendly bustle of workers and volunteers, and the sense of community that it creates.

A young ex-resident explained that she had stayed at The Hyce on two occasions, and had used Centrepoint, Soho, and a range of London hostels. She was very positive about the project, without ignoring the tensions which arise from overcrowding, boredom or depression among the residents. Accommodation can be offered to 10 girls and boys, although, in an emergency, more floor space can be found. No one is ever sent away. The residents have to be out of The Hyce by 10 a.m. on weekdays, but there are no limits on the length of stay. Communal evening meals are provided and residents learn to shop and budget.

Most of the residents are likely to live close to the poverty line for much of their lives and so thriftiness is an essential survival skill. Budgeting, swapping and altering clothes and learning to shop wisely form central elements in the project. Assistance in dealing with the DHSS, job centres, solicitors and other agencies is also given. A furniture exchange is organised for those who are rehoused. A solicitor, health visitor, housing specialist and careers officer come at regular intervals.

The day centre is open from mid-day until mid-evening. It is used as a meeting place by young mothers. A crèche allows for discussions on child care and development. Art and music workshops are held and trips are arranged to play football, or use the sports or swimming facilities in the town. Many of the users come from Hatfield and the surrounding districts. Some, however, are runaways or have moved from as far afield as Scotland. The users are getting younger and the number of teenage referrals is also on the increase.

More than 3,000 people have used the project over the

years. It is a mark of its success and value that many ex-residents come back from time to time after they are established and have settled, sometimes with their own families. They now offer support to the youngsters who come to the project. Above all, the intention is to offer love and care and create a family environment. To a considerable extent this is achieved.

The project is managed by the National Children's Home (NCH) who took it over in April 1985. It was originally set up in association with Hertfordshire County Council who remain one of the main sources of funding. NCH provide administrative and financial support and a valuable source of information.

The methodology appears to be very informal and flexible, but the apparently informal way in which needs are met, advice dispensed and potential crises averted belies the skill of the staff.

Informal advice is backed up, when appropriate, with an appointment system. Staff have found that a waiting period is valuable in helping young people to discuss their feelings both with staff and other users. Reviews of the progress of residents take place every few months.

Staffing

There are three full-time workers and a warden has just been appointed for The Hyce. Three community service volunteers do a stint at Bridges and there are about six regular volunteers. Tolerance, patience, friendliness and a sense of humour are considered necessary for the job.

Future plans

Because of the need for long-term accommodation in an area where the local authority does not house single young people, links have been developed with local housing associations and short-life property has been acquired. The aim is to provide a three-stage system of housing including:

● The Hyce: Emergency 'crash pad'
● a 26-bed hostel
● 10 houses providing community living.

The idea is that people should be able to move between the three stages according to their needs. Attempts are also being made to contact all other relevant projects in Hertfordshire so that they can meet, exchange news and share ideas, knowledge and resources. A system of support for those who have acquired accommodation is being developed, using volunteers. There is also a befriending service for young people in digs. It is intended to extend this service and, if possible, to acquire a shop in the centre of town for fund-raising, advice services, and coffee and snacks for young people. Bridges places high priority on extending its links with the local community. To this end, they are also campaigning for free access to recreation facilities for those who are unemployed or on long-term Supplementary Benefit.

2 *West End Co-ordinated Voluntary Service* The West End agencies in London include a significant number of projects offering advice and counselling services, emergency accommodation, hostels, health services and long-term accommodation through housing associations and voluntary schemes. Co-operation and collaboration are considerable and much more developed than in provincial cities.

WECVS administers a grant from the Voluntary Services Unit of the Home Office to some central London agencies concerned with homeless single people. The central office of WECVS, through the co-ordinator, is responsible for the distribution of this grant, although the amounts involved are determined by the VSU.

Member organisations aim to develop a comprehensive service for the homeless in Central London, and, to a considerable extent, achieve that aim. WECVS, in addition to funding, aims to facilitate good practice in member agencies, by encouraging them to monitor their own service. This area of work could be extended if WECVS were itself better funded. One agency thought that there was too little sharing of knowledge and experience. A hostel support workers' scheme has been set up to provide much needed relief cover for overworked hostel staff. It also allows hostel staff to be released for training and ensures a flow of ideas between hostels through the overview of the two workers.

Recently WECVS has been looking at ways of extending

daytime facilities in Central London and wishes to extend existing provision to weekends and bank holidays. A feasibility study was set up with funds from the Housing Associations' Charitable Trust to look into the possibility of providing capital for such a scheme.

WECVS also provides a base from which joint representations can be made, and responses developed collectively, to government policies.

While in theory WECVS should be a powerful advocate for the agencies, its position is weakened by inadequate resources. Where specific needs have been identified by member organisations and discussed in WECVS, leading to the development of auxiliary or follow-on services, the projects appear to work well together.

Conclusions

There are considerable tensions in the voluntary sector between agencies providing accommodation. There are differences of view on how far they should plug the gaps which result from the closure of statutory provision, or from the failure of statutory agencies to take on their legal responsibilities. Some agencies see their role as continuing to provide a service, not questioning why the need arises nor acting to deal with the cause. Others consider that this weakens their own attempts to raise standards and improve the nature and quality of provision for young people. Of one thing there is no doubt: without an effective response from the voluntary sector, there would be considerably more street youth than the numbers we have today.

5
HEALTH ISSUES FOR THOSE ON THE STREETS

Health problems are the inevitable result of a street-based existence. Aches and pains, coughs and bronchial infections are a consequence of our inclement weather and exposure to the elements. Foot infections, septic sores and minor ailments are also common. A few suffer complications from drug and alcohol abuse. Malnutrition, or an inadequate diet, is commonplace among those who live permanently on the streets or at minimal Supplementary Benefit levels.

Stopover, Edinburgh, reports 'Many of the residents suffer from bad health probably as a result of unstable lifestyles. Most common are skin complaints and stomach pains. Some of these may be due to bad nutrition over a long period, and certainly eating habits are generally not healthy. Some may also be anxiety-related. Many residents appear listless, cannot sleep and are generally tense.'

In Britain, registration with a general practitioner is dependent upon having a permanent address. A number of voluntary projects have arisen specifically to provide medical attention for those of no fixed abode. Two particularly notable initiatives are the *Great Chapel Street Medical Centre*, set up in 1978 to provide general medical services to the young people who drift about the West End of London, and the Friday night surgery run by *Kaleidoscope* in Kingston-upon-Thames as part of its all-night youth club. Both recognise that those with no fixed abode may be reluctant to go to local GPs or are not accepted by them. Both consider that the attitudes, approach and style of service are as important as the medical care they offer, and both projects arose from the recognition that homeless young people had medical needs

49

which were not being met. The content of the services varies substantially.

Great Chapel Street Medical Centre

Great Chapel Street has considerable sympathy for its patients but is firm about its prescribing policies. Situated in the West End, it has taken a firm stance about prescribing – no sedatives, tranquillisers or potentially addictive drugs are prescribed. Patients with alcohol and drug problems are referred to specialist agencies. This, the administrator feels, has been appreciated by the patients and enables relationships based on trust to develop. In seven years, the centre has seen over 5,300 patients and carried out 21,000 consultations. In October and November 1985, it saw between 25 and 40 new patients a week, plus up to 66 returning patients. It is open in the afternoons from 12.45 to 4 p.m. but has a 24-hour telephone contact seven days a week. It is not considered necessary to extend the surgery's hours since seven-day cover is available for emergencies. The centre no longer operates a rigid age limit as it is able to cope with the existing level of demand.

Most of the patients are under 35, more than half under 25. Most are sleeping out or in night shelters, although many also come from London hostels, bed-and-breakfasts and flats. Most hear about the services on the grapevine or in the shelters, day centres and hostels. (The informal grapevine is one of the most important means of communication for all projects.) The need for this centre has been clearly demonstrated and the service has developed in response to those needs. Psychiatric services are available, and a visiting psychiatrist holds a weekly session. A chiropodist has been appointed and there are plans to make Great Chapel Street the centre of footcare for the homeless. An occupational therapist is also being taken on to offer more possibilities in the care of psychiatric patients. The nurse also visits the hostels to give talks on first aid, contraception and health care. Research has been done on tuberculosis, epilepsy, foot problems and the psychiatric needs of the homeless.

Experience has shown the need for bed-rest to be offered to patients not ill enough for hospital admission. A sick bay has

COUGH
COUGH

therefore been established at Wytham Hall, which accommodates trainee doctors. Acute infections have been the main source of admissions, with foot problems second. The availability of the sick bay (used by 107 patients in its first year) has, it is felt, radically changed the scope of patient care at Great Chapel Street. The sick bay has extended the range of primary health care of the homeless. Staff also try to arrange appropriate accommodation on discharge. Funding comes from a variety of statutory and charitable sources, although changes in DHSS board and lodging payments are posing problems.

The administrator at Great Chapel Street feels that it would not be realistic or appropriate to expect GPs in general to respond to the needs of homeless people. Several reasons are put forward. It is particularly important to create the right atmosphere and to respond appropriately. The anti-social characteristics of some homeless people may elicit a negative approach from staff and patients in a GP surgery. Lack of understanding would, it is felt, inhibit the homeless from attending.

Staff at Great Chapel Street share tasks and there is a blurring of counselling and medical roles.

The centre operates on a very low budget of £21,600 which is heavily subsidised. Rent, heat and light are provided free, the nurse's salary is met from the Health Authority and the doctor is paid according to the number of patients seen, rather than the number registered. A great deal is being learnt from this project and alternative approaches to medical care for the homeless might well be tried in other cities.

Kaleidoscope

Established as a youth club in the late 1960s, Kaleidoscope quickly identified more specialised needs in Kingston, Surrey. It found that many young people who came to the all-night youth club were homeless or squatting locally. According to Kaleidoscope, as a result of repeated rejection over the years some found solace in alcohol or drugs, while others showed anger and violence. There was a substantial medical need which was not met by local doctors.

Kaleidoscope set up a well-equipped doctor's surgery

which is open at times convenient to the users of the centre. A registered mental nurse, state registered nurse and a doctor with psychiatric training run a no-appointments service and meet a wide range of physical and psychological needs. The nurses are full-time and the doctor comes on Friday evening for the surgery. The surgery is also part of West Middlesex Hospital Drug Dependency Unit and acts as the dispensing centre for South West London. Kaleidoscope has an excellent community-based approach to dealing with drug abuse which was commended by other projects.

Because of its youth work approach, Kaleidoscope is able to build up relationships with vulnerable young people before they become involved with drugs. Few addicts are willing to use hospital clinics or rehabilitation hostels outside their own area. Kaleidoscope offers a specialist service in the community on a residential, weekly or twice-daily basis. Forty people a day are treated on the methadone maintenance programme.

A residential hostel has also been opened, and has far more applicants than places. It was the only housing project seen which did not exclude drug users. Hostel residents also have other needs, including pregnancy, mental illness and the health problems which arise from life on the streets. It aims to provide an individual response to individual needs and it appears to be highly successful in that. The workers try to build on people's inner emotional and spiritual strengths. The Director, a Methodist minister, and staff who run the project have recognised the importance of stability in the lives of people who have unstable backgrounds. The décor, colour schemes, lay-out and equipment have all evolved from working with young people and in response to their needs.

Drug Addiction and the Hungerford Project

The rise in drug dependence among young people has particular implications for those involved in housing homeless young people, of whom they form an increasing proportion. Drug-dependent youth also make demands on the medical service – demands which doctors are not always able to meet. Government figures (which only include notified cases of addiction to certain drugs), have shown a 470 per cent increase in drug addiction amongst young people under the age of 21 between 1980 and 1984. Media efforts have drawn attention to the problems and highlighted the dangers, but, with existing resources, projects are unable to cope with the problem. As Glasgow District Council stated, 'There is a woeful shortage in the provision of adequate facilities for the treatment of addiction ... rehabilitation units and detoxification centres are virtually non-existent'.

The Hungerford Drug Project in London has seen the level of demand for the service increase dramatically in recent years, new client contact having risen by 50 per cent in 1983/4 (the most recent figures available). During that year, 3,829 contacts were made with the project, of whom 727 were new clients – an increase of 46 per cent. Half the clients were under 24, 18 per cent less than 20, 32 per cent between 20 and 24.

A quarter of new referrals were seeking support or counselling. Many of these had already experienced a period of rehabilitation or treatment at a hospital drug treatment centre, yet had relapsed into drug taking, or felt in danger of doing so. Thirty-three per cent of referrals sought help with detoxification or rehabilitation. Occasionally a need for psychiatric help was expressed.

The project depends on good medical back-up and has close links with in- and out-patient units at hospitals receiving drug users. Relationships with GPs are poor. Only one local GP is willing to co-operate with the project. Yet workers feel that, if every GP in London were willing to take on four drug users, working with them promptly, their medical needs could largely be catered for. As it was, most GPs were not willing to prescribe methadone as part of a detoxification programme. They referred users to drug clinics which were substantially over-subscribed so the addict would be asked to come with a urine sample every day for a week. Then he or she would be put on a waiting list for a month or more before receiving treatment. So someone who had taken the decision to come off drugs had to get over a vast number of hurdles. Given the chaotic lifestyle of most drug users, this often resulted in their continuing the habit rather than carrying through their initial desire to break with it.

Some clinics have an open-door policy, but lack of staffing means waiting lists for treatment. The project feels that the answer lies not in providing more specialised services such as Great Chapel Street, but in a change in the attitudes of GPs. Staff felt that the majority of new drug users would not be recognised in a doctor's surgery which was the appropriate place for treatment. Specialised services were necessary for more serious cases but inappropriate for the majority.

In a project where some medical and psychiatric knowledge are necessary, staff need time to develop their own skills and to extend their knowledge as new drugs appear. An increasing number of requests are now received by the project from professional workers wanting in-service training in drug problems. The DHSS has agreed to fund a training officer post in the coming year.

Medical care is also a feature at Blue Triangle in Glasgow, where nurses with a psychiatric training and knowledge of drugs are employed. Hygiene and personal health issues are discussed in the hostel. Girls go with staff to VD clinics, or ante-natal counselling, since pregnancy is used by some girls as a means of being housed. One of the 'home-makers' (volunteers who help the girls settle into their accommodation when they leave the hostel) offers a family planning service. Medical needs are substantial.

The project team for the Livingston hostel in Scotland recognises the need to have medical services available on site, as the team leader is a nurse, but few other projects mentioned this. Some projects have a very good relationship with a local GP. Without a good relationship the doctors will not come out in response to night calls. Shortage of staff in some hostels poses problems if a resident needs to be accompanied to hospital. Long-stay projects and housing associations encourage residents to register with a local GP.

Projects with a medical aspect depend upon a good working relationship with local health services. Funding questions are difficult to resolve for they often involve local and regional health authorities, charitable donations and capital grants toward the buildings.

More projects should take on board the medical needs of their clients and there is scope for innovative approaches to the medical needs of street youth to be established out of London.

6
EDUCATION AND TRAINING

Street-based projects in Third World countries pay attention to the educational needs of young people, particularly for those in their early teens and younger. Since education in Britain is compulsory until the age of 16, there is little evidence of projects specifically offering an educational service since that is considered to be outside their remit. The projects that receive persistent absconders from school seek to sort out their emotional and psychological, rather than educational, needs in the hope that they can be re-established into a secure home environment from which other activities, including schooling, may develop. All saw little point in forcing young people to return to a school in which they were totally disoriented or unhappy. No one learns against their will.

General Educational Provision

Long-stay residential projects offer a range of educational and sporting opportunities, while drop-in centres and day centres include such provision in their aims. All projects consider that the development of skills, so that the individual could live independently, is an integral part of the work. Most of the residential projects hold counselling sessions to evaluate the person's condition, needs and progress toward a permanent home. Such meetings are usually compulsory. More formal sessions on budgeting, managing money and practical skills such as paying bills are also held. A practical, problem-solving approach is used to develop skills necessary for dealing with the DHSS and housing departments. Cooking is also encouraged and some of the hostels for women offer cookery classes on site.

Projects such as New Horizon, Kaleidoscope and Bridges offer a range of activities, including art workshops, pottery classes, photography, history, literature, drama and music sessions. Shades discovered substantial musical talent and is therefore getting involved in a community arts project. These projects stress the importance of the activities programme for staff and residents getting to know each other. Visits to places of interest, and sports events as well as sporting activities using locally available facilities, are also encouraged. They include soccer, canoeing, ice skating and swimming. New Horizon has found a weekly video-making session very popular.

Activities are important to help unemployed youngsters pass the time and to foster local links which can be built upon when a permanent home is obtained. Blue Triangle holds sewing classes for its residents. The finished items are bought back from them and sold at fund-raising events for the hostel. Kaleidoscope is untypical in trying to meet the formal educational needs of residents. An education unit 'Magnet' has been established nearby with a tutor living on site. If, as a result of a breakdown or illness, someone has missed O or A levels, Kaleidoscope will try to find a specialist tutor to work with the young persons, so that exams can be re-taken. Kaleidoscope is not hindered by academic years, college time-tables or locations. Up to 30 people regularly use its educational facilities.

Some residents from Bina Gardens and Kaleidoscope also take formal classes at local further education colleges. The emphasis on terms and academic years, however, makes it difficult for some homeless people to fit into the timescale of courses. More flexible opportunities should be provided for young people to take up their education when their domestic circumstances allow. Closer contact between housing projects and education services is also desirable. There may be scope for encouraging 'open' and distance learning at hostels and housing projects. Open learning allows people to undertake some of their course at home, using self-study packages, with support from course tutors at a local college where necessary, and some group work or class contact if desirable.

It has the advantage of being flexible both in the style and time of delivery, and does not impose the isolation which can occur in learning through correspondence courses.

While the majority of homeless youngsters left full-time education at the earliest possible opportunity, Stopover, Edinburgh, found that more young people who would have liked to follow a course at the Further Education College were prevented from doing so by the Supplementary Benefit regulations which debar people in full-time education from benefit.

More than 90 per cent of the young homeless people are dependent on Supplementary Benefit because they are unemployed. Some gain access to Youth Training Schemes (YTS) but several projects will not encourage people to go to YTS. Particularly in Scotland, projects commented on the low esteem in which young people hold YTS because it does not help them 'to obtain a real job'.

Kaleidoscope was the only project seen which offers training for work. This is done on a small scale in the bakery and coffee shop. These two services do not cover their costs but are both therapeutic and instructive. Work experience is given on a one-to-one basis.

There is discussion among voluntary organisations as to whether projects should aim to keep young people mentally stimulated throughout the day or whether they should be free to spend their time as they choose. One project considers that offering night shelters to keep young people off the streets and day centres to keep them occupied is a wholly inappropriate response to young people's housing needs. Educational opportunity, mental and physical activities, however, help improve people's self-esteem, as well as alleviating the boredom of hostel life.

Information and Advice Services

A substantial number of projects offer information and advice on a range of issues arising from the housing need, though some merely refer young people to others for that service. Developing the young person's skills so that he/she can make effective use of advice centres is part of every project. Offering advice on welfare rights, and the legal issues arising from homelessness or housing matters, requires complex and specialist knowledge. Such services are well developed in London, but vary elsewhere. Not all projects can acquire the necessary knowledge and there is a danger of incorrect information being given when workers are not aware of all the complexities. The Piccadilly Advice Centre in London has committed time, money and human resources to the production of manuals to prevent other projects having to duplicate information. Shades produces a particularly good guide to provision in Manchester.

The PAC specialises in housing advice. At the time when the centre was founded, it was intended to have an advice centre or information booth at every London station for young people arriving in the capital. This scheme failed. British Rail did not support it, and it was found to be too expensive and impractical.

PAC takes a minimum of three months to train a new worker to know the sources of information and offer guidance to young people. It has been recognised that what is needed is a properly resourced single-door access to services for young people. In London PAC has assumed that role through being in the Piccadilly Underground subway which many young people are likely to pass through. It is absolutely vital that information should be accurate, reliable and up-to-date. Few projects are able to maintain that level of specialist information, counselling and guidance without a bank of local and national data.

One of PAC's main aims is to act as an information resource for other agencies. Information packs are produced for Crisis at Christmas and for Capital Radio Christmas Line. Statutory and voluntary agencies use the telephone information service, the demand for which has risen by 25 per cent. As a result of the work, detailed information manuals have been drawn up and are updated regularly. The *London Hostel Directory* giving information on more than 300 hostels is published by PAC.

There is a desperate need for a computerised database which can be made readily available and regularly updated. If someone comes into a London advice centre wishing to go to another city or a smaller town and wanting to know what facilities are available for young people, it should be possible to give him/her an answer. The information is not generally available. PAC are in the process of putting their hostel directory on computer, but that is a small step forward. Most of the information available is fragmented and remains in the hands of advice workers and individual projects.

Resources should, it is felt, be found to develop advice and information services in every region, with local centres in the towns where young people become homeless. These centres should provide information on housing projects, learning and training opportunities, as well as welfare rights. The management should be friendly and the centres should be open at times convenient to young people. In recent years, Britain has expanded its general advice services through Housing Aid Centres and Citizens Advice Bureaux, but few have the specialist knowledge of young people's needs.

Preventive Education

As a result of its activities, the Piccadilly Advice Centre feels that young people throughout Britain should be made more aware of the issues involved in leaving home, sources of information about how to make the transition, what options might be available, the problems which could arise, how to cope in a crisis and where to go for assistance.

The *Leaving Home Project* was set up by PAC to help young people recognise and consider the choices they face in leaving home, and the factors which limit those choices, to encourage discussion in schools, to assess what teaching materials are available, to evaluate how they are being used and whether they are appropriate.

Teaching about housing, when the subject is studied in schools at all, focuses on the technicalities of housing law, DHSS regulations and mortgages. What seems to be lacking is discussion of what is likely to happen in practice, and the emotional and personal stresses which arise. Young people also need to learn skills to achieve a successful transition to independent living. How to cope with loneliness, make new friends, deal with neighbours – all of which, it was felt, deserve attention in schools.

The Leaving Home Project studied the materials which were available. A useful catalogue of resources for teachers and youth workers entitled *Finding Out About Housing* has been produced and the project has identified the wide range of resources including teachers' packs, books, games, films, videos and tape/slide presentations available for use in schools, youth clubs or hostels.

However, while there is a wide range of materials, the project was concerned that no one knew how to evaluate them, or whether they meet teachers' needs. Indeed no one knew whether materials produced by housing agencies were being put into use at all. The Leaving Home Project, with minimal staff and resources, has tried to answer some of these questions, to find out what is being used, and how, and whether what is available is appropriate. One of the problems which housing agencies face is that those who are willing to fund publications in this field are not usually prepared to provide the additional resources needed to pilot these materials. They are less concerned with quality than with the numbers that can be distributed.

An attempt will be made to evaluate a new training manual entitled *Leaving Home*, produced by the Scots Group and Intermediate Treatment Resource Centre in Glasgow. This is being distributed to all local education authorities and given widespread publicity.

Little is known about what materials work best in the classroom and the teaching methods appropriate for this sensitive area. By designing courses for teachers and working with them to develop practice, the Leaving Home Project hopes to establish some useful models. However, because of inadequate funding in 1985 the project has only one full-time worker which severely limits its effectiveness. At least two more are needed to be able to follow up *Leaving Home* and assess its effect. The project was severely hampered by the lack of financial support from the Department of Education and Science and regrets that the DES has not endorsed the inclusion of *Leaving Home* in general studies in schools. It appears that few schools have included the issue in their studies to date.

The Young Homelessness Group based at CHAR also tries to raise public awareness of homelessness among the young and to encourage young people to consider the issue before they are directly affected. Nationally, the group brings together representatives of housing, youth and social services agencies. They bring a broad perspective to the subject and exchange information. A leaflet entitled '18 Years Old and No Place to Call Home' has been produced and is to be followed by a series of conferences on the new Supplementary Benefits legislation and other related issues.

Workers from PAC, Shades and Kaleidoscope go into schools. The first two discuss leaving home and homelessness. Kaleidoscope talks about drug abuse. It also produces a leaflet for parents and uses the surgery as a base for health education ranging from contraception to child care.

Conclusions

Educational issues arising from the needs of street children deserve to be given priority in the general studies in school. Practical work needs to be done with young people to evolve imaginative responses to their needs which do not appear to be met at present. Some projects would also benefit from an evaluation of their educational provision to see whether it is the most appropriate. Further links with local education authorities could also be made in order to overcome the barriers of college timetables and academic years. This is being achieved in some places through the 'Open College' or 'Open Tech' schemes. No one mentioned using distance-learning techniques, computer-based learning or open learning combining personal and college-based study, which may also be worthy of investigation.

7
SOCIAL NEEDS

There is an ideological conflict between voluntary agencies over the extent to which projects for homeless young people should concern themselves with social activities. Those who see homeless young people as ordinary youngsters needing accommodation, consider the provision of social activities no more or less desirable than for young people in general.

The *Soho Project* (a street based agency in London) has expressed concern that a 'significant minority of the homeless youngsters seen ... are addicted to gambling or fruit machines'. They are concerned that 'when almost every café, fish and chip shop and public house contains a gambling machine it is little wonder that some youngsters become addicted'. The project is playing a role in highlighting the potential hazards from the proliferation of such machines and is trying to understand and explain the nature of the problem and how it can be overcome.

Homelessness involves more than the absence of a roof. It is, or may become, a part of the search for support in the difficult transition from a life based on the home, family and/ or institution to one of independence.

Survival on one's own and the acquisition of temporary shelter are seen by a considerable number of agencies as the base from which someone's physical and mental well-being can be provided for, before their long-term needs are met. As one agency described it: '10–15 per cent of those at the night shelter are seeking more than a bed. They bring their home-lessness baggage with them. ... Even for those with a flat or job available, 10–15 per cent screw it up, for they still have other issues to resolve.' In the words of one young hostel resident: 'I prefer this place to the shelter 'cos this has less rules. I wants a roof, a bed, some company and money eventually. .... It's great here. You can stay up late and play music.' Some hostels commented on the disruptive effects of boredom and alienation when there is no social provision.

Social support is considered necessary by some organisations in the middle phase after leaving home and before becoming established in independent accommodation. Other agencies would reject this approach, seeking an immediate long-term solution to the housing crisis. They would leave it to the young person to develop his or her means of social support.

Drop-in centres, day centres and youth clubs are valuable in providing emotional space where young people can work out their ideas, beliefs and problems in a safe environment. There will be other people to talk to in friendly surroundings.

In some centres run by voluntary agencies, privacy is respected to a greater extent than in the public sector and if individuals want to lose themselves in the crowd, that will be accepted. The most such projects expect when someone comes through the door for the first time is to be given a name. They will not necessarily check its accuracy.

Several of the projects visited offered a bridge between a youth club and counselling service. They gained part of their funding from the Youth Service. There was a feeling that traditional youth clubs could do more to attract homeless young people and respond to their needs. Involvement in a youth club could also help to foster links with a local community which may be important for a young person waiting to be rehoused.

As long as young people are forced out of hostels and shelters on to the streets during the day, there will continue to be a need for social activities at day centres. For those newly homeless, day centres also offer a place to meet people and find out what is available to them. The grapevine is still the most effective communication network.

There are too few day centres offering satisfactory facilities for homeless youngsters and the lack of provision is particularly serious in London.

A valuable role can be played by general services for the young linking educational, social and advice services. When these are well developed, they encourage past users to keep contact, act as a reference point where people can return if the need arises, and offer an informal support system for young people. The danger lies in potentially setting the homeless apart from the rest of society, so that they lose contact with their peer group. Homeless people are vulnerable, however, and should have access to a suitable range of services.

In reality, available social activities are limited. Projects offer a meeting place, usually a cheap cup of coffee or food and a friendly, non-judgemental environment. Most are only open for a short time during the day and that mainly on weekdays. Only those with organised educational activities have a developed social programme. Inside hostels provision is based mainly on a communal TV lounge. A few also have a pool table or table tennis. Some make trips outside their area and encourage activities appropriate to a family, e.g. birthday celebrations. Where sports equipment is used, money for it has to be raised specially.

A difference of view about the need for social provision emerged between the London-based agencies and those in the rest of the country. This is in part because the London agencies are stretched in terms of human and financial resources and do not consider social provision part of their brief. It also reflects differences in the availability of local amenities. In London there are plenty of sports centres, cinemas, folk clubs, cafés and pubs, although they may be expensive. Long-stay hostels in the north of England and Scotland feel it important to generate a family atmosphere and the social provision encourages people to join in.

8
INCOME-GENERATING ACTIVITIES AND EMPLOYMENT

Anyone living at the margin has to acquire street skills to survive. Since the majority of homeless young people are also unemployed, it is necessary to acquire the skills needed to deal with the DHSS, housing departments and unemployment benefit offices. In April 1984 Youthaid, a national voluntary organisation for young, unemployed people claimed that there were 349,374 young people among the long-term unemployed.

Unemployment creates stress in the family and this, together with insufficient levels of income support for the unemployed, contributes to youth homelessness. The SCSH's *Think Single* report showed that lack of, or low, income delayed independence – three-quarters of the lower income groups staying longer at home. When unemployment affects several members of the family, young people often feel forced to leave to try to find work, or themselves contribute to the domestic conflict and are encouraged to leave.

The Piccadilly Advice Centre says that most young people who had come to London are genuinely seeking work. They lack information on the availability of employment in the South East and do not appreciate the fact that, although there are more jobs available in the London area, there are considerably more people seeking work, so their chances of getting a job remain slim.

Even if they get a job, however, housing is likely to be a problem for all but a privileged few. A good quality hostel costs at least £50 a week. Most young people cannot earn enough to cover that cost and provide for fares and meals.

Many hostels have to subsidise employed young people so that they can have a roof over their heads.

Housing projects are placed in difficulty because of the funding implications of taking on both employed and unemployed residents. The projects aim to balance their budgets with the amounts paid by DHSS for board and lodging for homeless residents. Because of the low wages paid to young people most employed homeless youngsters cannot afford to pay as much as is paid on behalf of the unemployed by the DHSS – that is, sufficient to cover the cost of accommodation in a reasonable hostel.

All projects, therefore, have differential rates for employed and unemployed residents with, paradoxically, the employed paying the lower amount. Since hostels and housing projects balance their budgets on the basis of maximum occupancy at DHSS rates, there is a disincentive to housing employed people. There appears to be no evidence that employed young people are actually turned away because of their low income. Whenever a roof is offered to an employed youngster, however, the project has to raise the difference between what they pay and the DHSS rates. This has to be obtained from other sources such as donations or fund-raising efforts. Bina Gardens charges only £25 a week for employed residents and tries to ensure they have £25 for fares and incidental expenditure. Only one project specifically discourages young people from seeking work. That project lays emphasis on attending long-term further education courses or other training. This anomaly will not be resolved merely by reducing the levels of housing benefit and board and lodging payments. Housing projects already have to raise a substantial proportion of their revenue and capital costs from charitable and other sources, since the income from residents does not cover costs.

Employment with tied housing is not generally considered suitable for young people, for if their previous housing record was bad they may be unable to maintain the house or job, and can end up back on the streets.

None of the projects have considered developing employment opportunities linked to the provision of housing, for that reason. UJIMA use Manpower Services Commission (MSC) schemes and employ young, otherwise unemployed, workers to improve the standards of their premises and bring short-life housing up to standard for letting. There is no relation between those who do the work and those offered housing. There may be scope for setting up a task force of young people who are trained to improve properties which they then live in but it can only be a partial contribution.

Some community youth schemes in the United States and Canada have incorporated housing with employment and may be worthy of further investigation. On the whole, agencies express scepticism at the idea, considering it to be an unnatural development with all the problems attendant to living on the job.

There appear to be no projects which combine training workshops with small-scale housing initiatives. These might also be developed in conjunction with housing association schemes.

Solutions must be found to the disincentive effects on young people caused by wages which are too low to cover the cost of a decent hostel. Cutting Supplementary Benefit levels and forcing people to move from place to place is not the answer. For many young people, having a job signifies opportunity. Young people increasingly feel that it is an opportunity they are being denied. When people have no housing and no earned income, their whole life begins to fall apart. The social and economic costs of that tragedy are not measurable, but prevention by adequate housing policies and family support must be a better use of resources than the alternative of paying health and social welfare services to pick up the pieces.

9
THE ROLE OF THE
STATUTORY SECTOR

The overview of street youth in Britain (Chapter 2) suggested that British society is inconsistent in its attitudes to young people and that this is exemplified by the lack of a cohesive government strategy for housing them. Legislation affecting young people has evolved piecemeal over a long period and so lacks a clear perspective. A young person may live away from home with parental permission between the ages of 16 and 18, and above the age of 16 may be entitled to Supplementary Benefit, and board and lodging or housing benefit. While able to leave home and claim benefit, however, legally between 16 and 18 they have not reached the age of majority and are in a state of limbo. Landlords may be reluctant to offer a tenancy until the person is 18, believing that 'a minor' cannot be sued for rent arrears, and they may require a parental guarantor for the rent.* Few local authorities will offer a tenancy to anyone under that age, although some are now taking young people on their waiting lists.

The Housing Act 1985

The Housing Act 1985 (Part III) placed responsibility for housing homeless people firmly within the remit of local authorities. Young people (and single people in general) have traditionally been given the lowest priority for housing and some authorities will not even allow under-18s to register on the housing waiting list. The purpose of the 1985 Act, how-

---

* See papers by the Children's Legal Centre to show the way the law affects children at different ages.

ever, was to ensure that local authorities offered advice and assistance to *anyone* who was homeless or threatened with homelessness.

The Act makes no specific reference to young people, but it identifies some who are considered to be in 'priority need' of accommodation. This includes those who are 'vulnerable as a result of old age, mental illness or handicap or physical disability or other special reasons', and who have not made themselves intentionally homeless. Housing authorities are also required by law to take account of guidance from the Secretary of State.

Such guidance is laid down in Codes of Guidance which outline the procedures to be followed by local authorities in implementing the Act. The Codes state that 'Authorities are also asked to have particular regard to those who are vulnerable and do not come into the previous categories' and in particular 'that it would be appropriate under this heading for authorities to secure that whenever possible accommodation is available for ... homeless young people who are at risk of sexual or financial exploitation'.

While Codes of Guidance are not legally binding, failure to follow such guidance may provide grounds for challenging a housing authority's decision. The Act and the Codes are open to widely differing interpretations and the practice of local authorities in dealing with single homeless young people bears this out.

Most councils, according to Shelter in its report *Make Room for Youth* are reluctant to house people under the age of 18 and insist that they return to their family homes. Yet the Minister for Home Affairs and the Environment in Scotland, Mr Michael Ancram, speaking at a Shelter conference in 1984 said, 'I firmly believe that local authorities have it in their powers under existing legislation and guidance to provide an effective response to the problem of homeless young people'.

Although local authorities have the powers, Shelter's evidence suggest that very few fulfil their responsibilities as outlined in the Codes. Some directly exclude applications for housing from young people under 18, referring all homeless under-18s to bed-and-breakfast establishments, with no proper assessment of their requirements or any intention of rehousing them in the future. Others are effectively excluded by being placed on waiting lists so long, and with so few priority points, that they have no realistic hope of being housed. Shelter goes so far as to say that the examples they have collected 'amount to an abdication by these authorities of their responsibility for dealing with all cases of homelessness. . . . The majority ignore even the most basic provision of the Act, that each applicant should have a thorough and individual assessment of their case, and apply only the most restrictive interpretation of the law.'

The gap between demand for local authority housing and available supply is shown by information from Glasgow. The authority's Working Group on Homeless Young People asked each area housing office to identify the demand from young people and make proposals for dealing with it. Glasgow has a very good record compared with other authorities and yet, while 181 16- and 17-year-olds were housed in Anniesland area alone, there were 1,414 young people from 16–25 on the waiting list. In the South area of the city, 151 single people under 25 were allocated housing in 1984 out of 721 on the waiting list. In Drumchapel, young people now form the biggest group requiring housing, with 419 on the list. Allocations in the first nine months of 1985 were significantly lower than the previous year. However, positive policies are being adopted. Anniesland intends to introduce a 25 per cent quota in all multi-storey flats for people under 25, to establish 20 self-contained flats and encourage existing tenants to take lodgers. Intensive housing support will be offered to young people who may be vulnerable. In Drumchapel, co-operation between social workers and the Housing Department has resulted in a proposal to form a joint support group which would, among other things, provide advice and counselling about the responsibilities of tenancy, and maintain contact concerning benefits, homemaker support and other services. New management policies are being considered including conversion of properties to form furnished bed-sits with caretaker/warden support, furnished flats for shared occupancy and community support from tenants' associations.

This demonstrates that, since the Act is loosely drafted, housing authorities which so choose can implement positive

71

policies toward 16–18-year-olds, on the grounds that all young people who are homeless are vulnerable. Glasgow, Newcastle, Liverpool and Ipswich are known to have accepted this responsibility. Manchester and Lewisham have stated policies which reflect a commitment to act, but have not yet been able to make the resources available to implement them. Lewisham co-operates closely with the voluntary sector and assists it with funding. Manchester also hopes to secure a range of provision in association with voluntary bodies and housing associations, but, in view of the financial implications, is urging that the needs of the single homeless in cities be recognised by central government through the rate support grant.

In Edinburgh it has taken several years for the local authority to face up to its responsibilities and Stopover notes that when the hostel was founded relations with statutory bodies were not good, and the climate of opinion was hostile to the needs of this group of youngsters. Now in its fifth year of operation, relations have improved. Problems arise if, after eight weeks, someone has not been placed and the council is not accepting responsibility. A certain amount of brinkmanship then takes place which, although disconcerting to the person in question, is usually resolved eventually.

It is worth outlining in some detail the approach taken by Glasgow, which appears to be the most comprehensive to date. Whilst it still has some flaws, staff are aware of them and doing their best to overcome the problems.

In Glasgow the challenge to house all homeless young people has been taken up by the city council which now has a 24-hour homeless person's unit, staffed in three shifts. Overnight accommodation is provided following a brief investigation of the young person's background, before referral to the Housing Department for assessment and counselling on the following day. The unit considers that there is no reason for homeless young people to be on the streets.

However, since there is no direct-access hostel accommodation, Glasgow's policy still relies very heavily on bed-and-breakfast provision until council accommodation can be found. The authority is committed to phasing out the use of such premises and in the interim has a worker who liaises once a fortnight with young people who live in bed-and-breakfast accommodation. She also looks at the quality of provision. Plans are being made for a hostel on similar lines to Stopover in Edinburgh.

Glasgow aims to house young people in the areas they come from or which have relevant services, and is involving area offices in trying to improve their record. With many young people on waiting lists, however, a number do become homeless. Their reception in local offices varies, and having been received by the Homeless Person's Unit some young people are placed in bed-and-breakfast accommodation for more than six months, waiting for a place of their own. Provision depends significantly on the area sought, and, until recently, young people tended to be placed in 'hard to let' properties resulting in problems such as drug abuse, vandalism and violence. Attempts were being made to solve these problems in discussion with area offices and to develop 500 furnished flats in mixed communities by March 1986. Some of these will be for young people who have difficulty obtaining furniture grants from DHSS. Regrettably, there is no monitoring of the effectiveness of Glasgow's provision for young single people.

There is much to be learnt from the experience of those authorities where statutory responsibility for housing young people has been accepted. But even the Glasgow experience makes no provision for those from outside the district, who are referred back to their own area or to a voluntary project.

The few local authorities visited were clear that where the need is for more than housing, there should be a social work input. This was endorsed by projects working with local authorities, but often presented problems because of the division between city and county (or in Scotland regional) responsibilities.

Where a young person suffers from drug addiction, alcohol abuse or comes within categories accepted as vulnerable (e.g. pregnant girls), local authority responsibility is clearer. Glasgow has produced an 'interim statement on drug abuse'. It specifies that the district council sees its main responsibility in the field of housing and feels that 'it is essential that housing department staff ... have an understanding of the problems associated with drug abuse' because of their implications for housing management policies. The council has a policy of providing group tenancies for ex-psychiatric patients who are able to live in the community and is considering the provision of group tenancies for ex-drug addicts who are recovering from their addiction.

Responsibility for Young People in Care

Young people under the age of 18 (17 in Scotland) may be taken into care, or received into voluntary care, if it is felt that proper care cannot be exercised at home. The person may stay in care until the age of 18, where he or she should be given some help in preparation for independent living.

Social workers and residential staff offer assistance to young people from care to get accommodation on leaving. Relations between young people and their social and residential care workers vary, and, as was shown in Chapter 2, the help is not always effective or sufficient to enable them to make a successful transition to independent living. Housing projects see a disproportionate number of young people from care. Project staff and young people from the National Association of Young People in Care (NAYPIC) feel strongly that young people coming out of care should be given particular assistance and support in moving to independent accommodation, so that they do not end up on the streets. Authorities should look at the types of management structure which may be appropriate and the best ways of supporting new tenants.

Projects are also critical about the ending of responsibility for young people in care at 18. Not all young people are ready for independent living at that age. But residential homes and independence projects usually cease to receive local authority funding for the young person and cannot cover their costs with housing benefit and social security payments. So contacts are often severed completely at 18.

The needs, it is felt, differ from one individual to another, and to cut off support totally at what is considered an arbitrary date is inappropriate to the needs of some young people. It is felt that organisations should have a certain amount of flexibility to continue to support young people from care until they can establish themselves with a chance of success.

Bosco House Children's Home commented that to do

effective work with difficult youngsters needs a long time, yet some placements of 16- and 17-year-olds are made for less than a year which is insufficient to prepare them for independent living. Such provision would never be cheap and local authority cuts have been severely felt. Central government, it is felt, should review the law regarding young people from care, and look at ways of making the transition from full-time care to independence less dependent simply on a date, namely the person's eighteenth birthday.

Social workers in Manchester recognise that young people leaving care need considerable support and feel that 'after-care' was the 'area most neglected in our work with youngsters leaving care'. They stressed that 'although limited, the local authority has some responsibilities under sections 27, 28 and 29 of the Child Care Act 1980'. They felt that in respect to housing, Manchester youth does fairly well and the Housing Department is sympathetic to the need for independent accommodation for those coming out of care. They do, however, feel that insufficient attention has been paid to problems of isolation and the need for relationships to be built up in the area in which the person is to be housed. Continuing contact with the residential home as well as support in sorting out bills, coping with repairs and budgeting are also recognised as important. How far improvements have been made in practice requires further study.

The problem is also recognised by the House of Commons Social Services Select Committee in its report on *Children in Care*. The committee stressed the need for local authorities to give far greater support to young people leaving care. It also proposed that the Housing (Homeless Persons) Act 1977 should be amended to give young people leaving care a statutory right to be housed by local authorities provided that they are homeless, or threatened with homelessness. Their comments are equally applicable to the Housing Act 1985 (Part III) England and Wales. Shelter and CHAR have been advocating such a change for all homeless young people.

Homeless Young People and Social Security

Access to housing for young people is substantially affected by the way in which particular local authorities interpret the law. However, government policy towards the payment of Supplementary Benefit also has implications for homeless youth (since most homeless young people are also unemployed) and for the projects themselves (since they receive a considerable part of their funding through benefit payments).

Young people may claim Supplementary Benefit if they have no other income and are available for work. The level of benefit depends on whether the person is categorised as a 'householder' (i.e. living in his own house, flat or bed-sit) in which case they receive a higher rate of payment; or as a 'non-householder' (e.g. if sharing a flat, staying with friends or at home); or whether they receive the board and lodging allowance which is paid to young people living in hostels or bed-and-breakfast accommodation and is supposed to cover rent, plus allowances for meals and personal expenses. In fact, certainly in London, the payments are hopelessly inadequate to meet living costs.

(a) The Board and Lodging Regulations

In 1985, the Government made fundamental changes in the regulations governing payments for board and lodgings. These changes actually legislate against young people and cause considerable hardship, on which almost all projects commented. Under the regulations, certain claimants under 26 can claim rent for bed-and-breakfast hotels for up to only eight weeks in Greater London, Birmingham, Manchester and Glasgow, two weeks in coastal areas and four weeks in other areas. When this time limit expires they receive a significantly reduced amount – the non-householder rate – and must leave the area and not return to claim benefit for six months if they are to obtain the full board and lodging benefit again. The implications for young people who do not have the opportunity to go home are all too obvious. Shades offer the example of a 20-year-old from Moston, who had to leave home and is homeless. She may claim for lodging house accommodation for eight weeks. If a tenancy or employment is not found in that time, she would be forced to move out of Greater Manchester, even if she had lived there all her life.

76

The nearest area in which she could claim benefit would be in Warrington. There she could claim for four weeks (provided she could find accommodation within the DHSS limits); then she would have to move again ... and again. So she would never be resident in an area long enough to qualify, or even register, for council accommodation and her links with the local labour market would be lost. As Nicolas Fenton, Director of Centrepoint, wrote in a letter to *The Times*, 'the assumption that young people will find jobs in two to four weeks is hopelessly unrealistic'.

The second change was to set nationally determined ceilings which are, on average, lower than the previous maximum levels. In London, the upper limit payable for bed and breakfast fell to £48.30, which significantly reduced the number of hotels in which claimants could afford to stay. The kind of accommodation available at those prices is at best squalid and over-crowded. At worst, it is non-existent.

Voluntary agencies have campaigned to show the injustice of the changes. While the Government aimed to reduce the rapidly escalating cost of bed-and-breakfast accommodation, which had risen by 143 per cent for those under 26 between 1982 and 1984, it was landlords and hoteliers who had profiteered from the rise in payments, not the claimants. Voluntary agencies accept that there was some abuse of the system, but, without exception, considered the response unduly heavy-handed.

Even the Government-appointed Social Security Advisory Committee questioned the basis on which the change had been made, stating: 'We are not convinced that the proposals as they stand are focused sufficiently on the problem area ... the revised proposals will cause hardship and difficulty to many people who have no option but to enter board and lodgings. ...'

The committee considered that there was no evidence of wide-spread abuse and recognised the danger of creating a class of homeless and rootless young people. They, too, felt that a long-term solution had to be found in housing policy itself.

No one knows the numbers affected. A DHSS study in the South East of England between June and August found that 28 per cent of claimants stayed at the same address when their entitlement ran out. Another 24 per cent stopped claiming benefit, one third went back to parents and one sixteenth to friends or relatives. However, central London agencies have felt the strain of being unable to find places for homeless young people to stay.

Increasingly, short-term hostels are having to offer long-term solutions for which they were not set up, or trained. The voluntary sector is bearing an intolerable burden.

New Horizon day centre suggests that in London it would be better to regulate the amount which could be charged for rooms of a certain standard. To be eligible for payments from the DHSS, hotels would have to comply with minimum health and safety standards. Young people deserve that protection and such an arrangement would also relate DHSS payments to the quality of provision.

Since most housing projects get a significant proportion of their revenue from DHSS payments, these changes have had a devastating effect on their budgets. Part way through the year, they are not in a position to revise budgets to any great extent and have limited room to manoeuvre without reducing bed spaces and cutting staff. Most are faced with having to raise an increasing proportion of their revenue from donations and special effort, which is extremely time-consuming and often has to be done by project staff over and above their normal duties.

(b) DHSS furniture grants

The offer of a local authority flat may, on the face of it, appear to solve a young person's housing problem. Yet, for single people on Supplementary Benefit, setting up home for the first time in unfurnished accommodation can involve protracted negotiation with the DHSS about furniture grants. The rules governing who gets a grant are complex and include reference to the person's health or disability, length of time on benefit, likelihood of continued unemployment and being able to prove 'that there is no suitable alternative furnished accommodation available in the area'. Delays in obtaining furniture grants and disputes over eligibility were mentioned by several projects. Bridges had established a furniture store so that young people did not lose the chance of a flat because they had no furniture.

(c) Housing benefit

Young people on low incomes who live in hostels, lodgings, or bed-and-breakfast, but who are not eligible for Supplemetary Benefit may be entitled to Housing Benefit, in which case they may receive a part-payment of their rent. Projects complained of delays in benefits being paid and difficulties in obtaining accurate assessments. Project workers all spent a considerable time liaising with the DHSS on behalf of residents, going to offices to assist a claimant and ensure that they obtained their entitlement. It is felt that the complexities of the system, and lack of sympathy with the plight of young people, make claiming a degrading experience for many.

The Role of Social Services Departments

As mentioned in Chapter 4, projects offering independence training for young people from care are critical of the role of social services departments in making placements and are wholly dependent on those placements to continue their work. Closure of children's homes results in fewer adolescents coming forward for independence training, and some independence training units are also closing. Staff feel that there is a need for assistance to be given to young people and that it should be possible to develop different ways of delivering the service. Projects are receiving only the most difficult referrals, and this, with a reduction in the numbers referred, can mean financial ruin.

Manpower Services Commission Involvement with Housing Projects

While there would appear to be considerable scope for MSC funding for housing improvement, job creation and YTS schemes, few of the projects visited mentioned involvement with the MSC. One suspects that this is partly because MSC training schemes require support and many of the projects could not afford to release staff for this purpose.

UJIMA is particularly interesting for the way it has developed a building work force funded partly by the MSC to renovate the properties licensed from local authorities. The schemes employ 176 long-term unemployed people and give them practical experience and training in the building trades. Trainees are enrolled on City and Guilds courses and the cost of training is borne by UJIMA. Skilled supervisors are employed by UJIMA, who also cover the cost of building materials. The MSC provides funding for trainees' wages, supervisors' wages and a contribution of £440 per trainee towards operating costs. This has made a substantial contribution to UJIMA's expansion programme.

Funding

Funding arrangements for housing projects are complex and involve a range of statutory, voluntary and charitable sources. Funding from central and local government is essential for the survival of almost all the projects visited, whether it be through grant aid or benefit payments to residents. Special project funding, Housing Corporation Finance, GLC support and Urban Aid have been particularly important in recent years.

The Scottish Council for Single Homeless report on *Hostel Funding* comments on several problems which are of concern to all projects:

● the difficulty of raising sufficient funds to start a project
● the distortion of a project's aims as a result of inadequate funding
● the insecurity of funding which means that a disproportionate amount of staff time was being spent on re-negotiating for funding
● much of the grant-aid available is short-term (1, 3 or 5 years) and often only partial.

Most projects are funded from several sources including grants toward capital costs, donations of buildings or contributions towards conversion of premises. All have problems in recovering their revenue costs, the largest contributor to which is the DHSS through payments to residents. Some projects receive funds from the Inner London Education Authority, or from Youth and Community Departments of local authorities.

The total cost of running the Hungerford Drug Project, for example, in 1983/4 was £79,000 of which £53,070 came from local authorities and £19,743 from DHSS and Home Office grants. The remaining income came from fund raising and charitable trusts. There are 19 potential sources of funding for drug projects and nine of these give to Hungerford. Funding is very insecure and the indications are that there will be a shortfall of £12,000 in the current year.

The Central London Teenage Project, meeting an undoubted need and doing pioneering work with 'runaways', is seriously under threat because, having assisted with the capital costs of the building, the DHSS now requires the Children's Society to raise the running costs in full. The Society had agreed to provide 50 per cent of the running costs of £135,000 and had hoped for DHSS support toward the rest. It is now trying to raise the money from other sources but, meanwhile, the project is vulnerable.

The Leaving Home Project in December 1985 had no guarantee of funding after the end of the financial year. Yet it, too, is doing important pioneering work, testing the effectiveness of educational materials. It was not even certain that there would be sufficient funds to write up the results of the research. The project has now been given funding by the London Boroughs Grants Unit. Projects generally consider the financial situation which they face to be scandalous.

When Hertfordshire County Council threatened to stop its funding for Bridges, the project was fortunate in gaining support from the National Children's Home: without it Bridges would have been forced to close. The back-up of a large national organisation and enormous effort by the staff not only enabled the project to survive, but has encouraged it to seek new sources of support in the local community. The county council has, in fact, maintained its support and actually increased the level. This is invaluable.

The instability and insecurity which projects face have an

effect on the morale of staff and often place an enormous burden on them, when they are already hard pressed to provide a service for which there is excessive demand. Insecurity over funding, and short-term funding, make planning for the future a luxury which most projects cannot afford. The Cambridgeshire 'drop-in' bus, for example, did not know in October 1985 whether it would continue beyond Christmas because the local authority had not confirmed its funding,* despite the fact that a replacement worker had just been appointed. Recruitment of staff is often made difficult because funding, and hence jobs, are on limited contracts; and projects can only take short-term leases on premises, which both increase costs and require them to move every few years.

Many projects faced with insufficient funding have to make choices about the nature of the service they offer, significantly limiting their effectiveness. Both Shades and Hungerford chose to withdraw their street-based services in the face of increased demand for advice and counselling. Both regretted having had to make that choice and, as soon as Hungerford was able to re-employ a street-based worker, the project and its clients benefited.

Projects also expressed concern about the way their services were assessed by potential funders, particularly government agencies. It was suggested that funding bodies are mainly concerned about numbers, rather than the service people receive, and whether it meets their needs. Notions of 'success' were not really appropriate. Yet the question arises, how should one evaluate the work done, for example, by an agency working with people on the street? This is an area which warrants further investigation. It was also suggested that, when under threat, and in the face of media scrutiny, agencies tended to withdraw into safe and known methods rather than to experiment.

What is often forgotten by management committees and funding bodies is that fund raising is now a highly skilled business requiring professional staff. It is not something which over-pressed project workers can or should take on in addition to, and to the detriment of, the service which they

---

* The funding has now been confirmed.

are providing. Yet that is increasingly what they have to do to survive.

Projects which are part of national organisations and projects such as Centrepoint, Soho, or Turning Point, which manages Hungerford, have separated their fund-raising responsibilities from housing provision and project work. They have been successful in their endeavours and so are able to devote more specialist staff to the job of raising money. Small may be beautiful, but it is also weak and insecure where a multiplicity of agencies compete for limited funds from the same sources. The view was expressed that where there were too few staff to raise funds, an effective management committee, directly involved in fund raising, could make the difference between survival and failure.

Annual funding is absurd for most projects. It creates instability and does not allow sufficient time to test the effectiveness of projects. A three-year rolling programme is much more appropriate.

Understandably voluntary organisations will not normally pursue a project if they are only offered part-funding and so would be unable to operate a service at what they considered to be an appropriate level.

A considerable amount of funding comes from within the voluntary sector itself and this should not be forgotten. The support, for example, of local projects and housing aid centres by Shelter, and adoption of projects by NCH or the Children's Society, all require a substantial commitment of personnel and resources.

The resource base for voluntary projects is inadequate to meet the demands placed upon it. Project staff are over-worked, too few in number and often based in inadequate premises which restrict the service they can offer. Yet the quality of what is provided often far outstrips the costs of provision.

Projects are being put under increasing pressure to raise more of their funds from non-statutory sources but this is both difficult and time-consuming. Evidence suggests that industrial and commercial sponsors are not rushing to put money into this area and the amount available from trust funds is limited. Since the voluntary sector does a lot of work on behalf of central and local government, central and local government should give it more money.

Conclusions

Projects were unanimously critical of government's failure to adopt positive policies to ease the housing crisis which faced young people and were highly critical of the impact of changes in funding policies on their work. They felt particularly aggrieved by the board and lodging changes, and the lack of consultation before these changes were made.

On the one hand, central government was trying to encourage the voluntary sector to take over responsibility for resettlement units and yet was unwilling to provide the funding, without which voluntary organisations could not possibly maintain the commitment and run the units effectively. The present Government's position was summed up by Sir George Young, Parliamentary Under-Secretary at the Department of the Environment, replying to an adjournment debate initiated by Mr Alfred Morris MP in the House of Commons on 20 December 1985. 'The Government,' he said, 'has accepted that the numbers of homeless people are increasing.' He stressed the social rather than economic causes of the increase and cited the fact that young people are leaving home earlier and in far greater numbers as one reason for this increase. Understanding the causes contributes little to their solution.

However, the Government is taking some action. In response to criticism of the unsatisfactory and expensive nature of bed-and-breakfast accommodation, the Secretary of State is consulting with local authorities about a draft memorandum which states the wide-ranging powers local authorities have for securing improved conditions. Attempts to raise standards and close places which are unsatisfactory must be matched by an increase in alternative affordable provision for young people.

Voluntary organisations consider the Government's response to be partial and inadequate. They seek a much more coherent strategy from the Government, taking account of the accommodation needs of young people and providing an appropriate level of financial support to fund an effective service. Organisations consider that improvements could be made in provision through closer working relations with central and local government agencies, and would welcome the chance to develop more approaches in partnership. While the resource implications are substantial, at present vast sums of money are being inefficiently spent in bed-and-breakfast hotels which are inappropriate and undesirable for many young people.

Some local authorities recognise the importance of supporting the development of good quality accommodation for young people in the voluntary sector. Voluntary organisations wish to see more priority given to the development of approaches in partnership, particularly in areas where local authorities have not taken up their responsibilities under the 1985 Act. To facilitate co-operation, and create a climate in which development can take place the Government should amend the Housing Act (Part III) for England and Wales and the Housing (Homeless Persons) Act 1977 for Scotland, and place a mandatory responsibility on local authorites to house all homeless young people.

10
THE ROLE AND FUNCTIONS OF THE VOLUNTARY SECTOR

Adaptation

Voluntary organisations provide shelter, care, counselling and support. They may offer education, both formal and informal, and training in life skills. A few offer training for employment or in work-related skills. In particular those working with homeless young people offer understanding, a roof – either temporary or permanent – security, and a more healthy environment than they would find on the streets. The strengths of voluntary organisations lie in their local commitments, their knowledge of users' needs and their ability to respond quickly when a new need is perceived.

Available housing for young people is very limited. In the past the emphasis was on institutional provision in night shelters and hostels. Generally it was short-term, insecure and sub-standard. It is wholly inappropriate today. Yet some voluntary organisations are locked into a policy which in theory opposes such provision while in practice continuing to provide it. Voluntary organisations which stagnate and continue to perpetuate substandard provision may be more inflexible than the public sector. Some continue to provide an inferior service because of inadequate funding. Voluntary organisations may offer alternative methods of providing a service; some find that they have to accept that any service is better than none.

Organisations with a substantial amount of out-dated accommodation are urged to adapt to today's needs, reappraise their strengths and examine the part they should be

playing. Large organisations tend to be less flexible for they have more substantial and long-standing commitments and may also be inhibited by their management structure. Young people deserve more than 'band-aid' to patch up their problems. They want to see effective solutions to issues which are beyond their control.

Voluntary organisations have been in the forefront of new developments in recent years, and some longer-established organisations have adapted quickly and effectively to meet new needs. The Children's Society's work at the Central London Teenage Project, and National Children's Home's with Bridges, are striking examples of agencies who have broadened their remit to provide housing for homeless youth.

Hostel developments have been the main growth areas, and several new initiatives are in the pipeline in Scotland. High quality, well-staffed, direct-access hostels appear to have a valuable role, particularly in providing emergency cover, but they must be part of a more comprehensive policy which voluntary organisations alone cannot and should not be expected to supply.

Voluntary projects should be flexible so they can change and develop new responses. Several of the West End projects have adapted considerably since they started, while others stagnated or closed as funding sources dried up.

Innovation

With limited resources and the short-term nature of funding, voluntary organisations have a valuable role to play in setting up relatively short-term experimental projects which test new methods, approaches or needs, before finding one which functions well and can be offered as a model to other voluntary agencies and statutory agencies alike.

The Central London Teenage Project's work is worth describing in full for it is the first 'runaway' project in Britain, is already identifying needs which have not previously been recognised, and is providing a response which may be copied elsewhere.

The Teenage Project offers a safe house and residential support for up to 12 young people under 17 (under 19 if in care) who have run away to London or are homeless in central London. It was set up in 1984 in response to concern from the West End agencies at the increasing number of young people who had run away from care and were seeking accommodation. No one knew how many were involved, but the Juvenile Bureau in Paddington dealt with 2,000 in 1980 and voluntary agencies saw 80 every three months.

There was general dissatisfaction with the requirement that young people be sent back to the problems they had run away from. Evidence showed that they ran away again and would not approach the relevant agencies for fear of being returned home. They were thus more streetwise and doubly vulnerable.

Meetings were held with voluntary and statutory bodies and in July 1984 a building was purchased. Staff were taken on the following Spring and after substantial delays in converting the premises, it opened in June 1985. The aims are:

- to provide a safe house
- to assess the needs of young people and provide a counselling service
- to investigate the circumstances which led to the person's arrival in London and seek acceptable long-term accommodation and care
- to return the young person to their home area or alternative placement as quickly and effectively as possible
- to evaluate present methods of helping young people
- to ensure the project does not harbour young people.

Since the house opened, 142 children have been in residence. Numbers have fluctuated and there has been no particular pattern, except that numbers increased when school started. The children come from all over England and Wales, Scotland, Eire and the EEC. Most, however, are from London and the South East. The numbers of boys and girls are roughly equal; 63 per cent come from a family home and 2 per cent from boarding schools. The youngest was aged 11, but they cluster between 14 and 16. The majority are referred by Westminster Social Services after being picked up by the police.

There is no limit on the length of stay, but on average residents have moved on within four days. The house is well furnished, warm and friendly, but the staff are honest with residents about the realities of life in London. They would be concerned if residents had to stay longer than 28 days. For some, supportive hostels are arranged if it is not possible for them to return home; 87 per cent do return home. For a persistent absconder, a placement in London is sometimes appropriate.

The project staff place particular emphasis on *listening* to young people. They do not accept everything they are told, but learn to be discerning and identify the real issues that have caused the young person to run away. Having gained their trust they give them time to sort out their problems. On admission certain procedures are followed. The staff try to obtain details of the person's real name, date of birth and where he/she has come from. They make no telephone calls without the resident's permission, and she/he is present when calls about them are made. The files are open and discussed and the approach is informal, but firm when necessary. The residents can always leave if they are not ready to co-operate. Some do. Some have been away for several months and it may then be difficult to stabilise them. However, time at the project helps young people to come to decisions about what they want to do.

Workers are aware that they still have a lot to learn about how to reintegrate young people into society, cope with the conflicts which arise between parents, agencies and young people, and try to find the best solutions.

Above all, they consider running away is a cry for help, a signal that traditional social supports are failing to meet the needs of a young person, distrustful of adults, but desperate for help and understanding. Lonely, depressed and disoriented, they may have run away from family problems or been thrown out of the family home. Fifteen per cent have suffered sexual abuse; others suffer physical or emotional abuse. Many have problems at school or in the children's home. The project staff particularly aim to listen to young people and encourage their parents, social workers and others to communicate.

This project depends entirely for its success on good working relations with relevant agencies. It is the first project which has drawn together in partnership the relevant agencies working in central London. These include Westminster

Social Services, Camden Social Services, the Juvenile Bureau, London Transport Police, Centrepoint Soho, the Soho Project, Alone in London, Salvation Army, Piccadilly Advice Centre and Bina Gardens.

A policy decision was taken in the beginning to restrict the number of referral agencies so that the project was able to cope. These will gradually be expanded. An agreement similar to that with the Westminster City Council is being drawn up with Camden and referrals will also be taken from London Transport Police. The possibility of extending access to agencies such as the Samaritans is being considered.

It is too early to say whether this model should be followed elsewhere in the UK, although American experience suggests that runaway shelters should be local to reduce isolation and provide support networks.

The potential for the future is extensive. The project has a great deal of material about young people's views and is currently identifying issues of particular concern such as sexual abuse and young people's attitudes to care.

It is hoped to be able to develop the family counselling and educative roles and there are a considerable number of legal issues to be resolved. The first aim, however, is to provide the service and learn from it. The researcher will follow up every child to find out what ultimately happens, maintain links with ex-residents and report back.

Evaluation systems are being set up so that workers can appraise their goals, and assess how far they are achieving their aims. To date they have a most impressive record.

Innovatory projects may not always be successful but this is a valuable part of the learning process. Where appropriate ways of working with young people are demonstrated, local authorities should be willing to take them on board. Central government should create a climate in which this can happen. Central and local government, as well as voluntary bodies, have a role to play in funding new initiatives, but this cannot be achieved with the limited staffing available to most voluntary projects at present.

Campaigning

For the majority of projects there is a dilemma between providing the service for which they were set up, and campaigning to change the climate of opinion. Also they must see that they do not just continue supplying the same limited service for ever.

Many project workers carry out campaigning in their own time, but are also able to use networks to share information and knowledge of more general problems as they arise. Work at the Teenage Project, for example, very quickly indicated problems of child sexual abuse. They are now monitoring the issue closely. Equally, hostel projects recognise the number of homeless youngsters coming from care and work has now begun on the prevention of this source of homeless youngsters. This is a proper role for voluntary organisations.

Co-operation

Voluntary agencies have considerable public support and when they work together, or in partnership with statutory agencies, they also have great influence. Projects such as Kaleidoscope, Great Chapel Street and Hungerford could not function without a working relationship with the police and social services. Such effective organisations result from a clear definition of the aims of the project; knowing what can and cannot be provided as part of the service; and mutual trust which arises from a recognition of the roles of the statutory and voluntary agencies. These projects also depend upon a degree of non-interference from statutory authorities so that they are free to work in areas where the legal position is unclear, but where human crises demand a humanitarian response.

Voluntary organisations have not been particularly effective in sharing knowledge about methods of working and good practice. The reasons are:

1 The isolation of voluntary projects in the regions and lack of contact with other projects with similar aims.

2 Lack of staff which makes it impossible to release staff for outside meetings and makes training an activity that many cannot afford.

Training should be built into projects as an essential part of the development of the service. Since voluntary projects are working directly with clients whose needs may change, staff need to evaluate the nature of what they offer and how it can be improved. The Teenage Project is to be commended for building locum cover into its work so that permanent staff can be released for that purpose.

Failure to share knowledge with other projects and to debate critically the problems faced is more difficult to explain. Lack of staff again is a factor. But less tangible reasons are to be found in the competition for power, influence, territory and relative size within the voluntary sector. The vulnerability of many small projects to closure through lack of funding, and concerns about competition, may lead people to safeguard their knowledge and professional skills. But several people from varying agencies said that they felt they would benefit from sharing ideas about methods of approach, dealing with different types of situation, how to evaluate the work and so on. Funding ought to be made available to facilitate the development and exchange of practical skills. Several joint working parties have been set up but it is rarely possible for staff from small projects to take part.

Stereotyping

There was a criticism from several specialised voluntary projects about being stereotyped by referral agencies who were then insufficiently selective in making referrals. UJIMA, for example, is a housing agency which provides independent accommodation with limited support. Yet it was said that social workers treated them as a 'dumping ground' for any black youth who needed housing. But UJIMA cannot take anyone who needs social work or psychiatric support. All projects in London said that if anyone with a drug dependence came to them they would be referred to Hungerford. Yet Hungerford is a counselling agency for those with drug-related problems and has no housing available. The fact is that there is no housing available for drug addicts since they are excluded from all the voluntary projects and have to find solutions in the bed-and-breakfast sector unless they are seeking rehabilitation.

On the other hand some agencies, particularly in London, make a deliberate effort to specialise and avoid duplicate provision. *North Lambeth Day Centre*, for example, which offers a service to single people, particularly alcoholic men, makes a considerable effort to refer any young people who drift into the centre to more appropriate agencies.

Detached Work

Few projects are doing any detached work on the streets. Hungerford and the Soho Project in London, and the Salvation Army in a limited way, were noted.

One of the original aims of the Hungerford Project was to carry out detached work on the streets of the West End of London. Recently a new project worker has been appointed to re-establish the street-based service. After only a few months his value was proved with a substantial increase in the number of contacts, particularly with new users and those in the 17 and 18 range who were unaware of Hungerford. Street work keeps the project in touch with the dangers facing drug users. In three months, 50 new contacts have been made and contacts re-established with people who had been unable to get to the project for some time. Such work is particularly valuable in building up trust.

Shades used to do detached work but, in the face of limited resources, is now concentrating on campaigning and the advice and activities it is able to offer centrally. So little is known about the way British street children and youth pass the time, the numbers involved and their needs that this should be a priority for investigation.

Staff and Volunteer Roles

The voluntary sector depends to a great extent on the energy, commitment and determination of its workers, both paid and voluntary. Their commitment often goes far beyond the call of duty, with the result that they may drain themselves, to the detriment of their own health and their clients' welfare.

Volunteers are used in a variety of ways by different projects, and most could not continue without them. At Stopover, Edinburgh, for example, volunteers are used to a limited extent, mainly to attend meetings between young people and statutory agencies, visit potential accommodation with them, and continue the contact and support after a home has been found. Staff want to increase the involvement of volunteers but recognise the difficulties.

It is now generally accepted that volunteers have a valuable role to play in providing the service – and not just making the tea! To be effective, however, and gain satisfaction, volunteers must be trained, and continuity requires the involvement of staff. Selection and support for volunteers are also considered to be important issues by Stopover, which is developing a policy for dealing with the greater use of volunteers. Increasing the use of volunteers will provide additional manpower and allow the professional staff time, for instance, for campaigning and public education. Hostel workers feel that volunteers are essential if there is to be a contribution to solving young people's housing needs and not merely to offer crisis provision. They know however that using volunteers will not actually save money, but on the other hand it will increase the human resources on which the hostel can call.

Projects should beware of becoming unduly dependent on a single key worker or project leader. Several of the projects in this study have developed an effective team approach so that all workers keep in touch with clients' needs and the day-to-day issues which require attention. Others are dependent on the enthusiasm, charisma or technical skills of one central figure, and one questions what would happen to the project and its clients if he/she became ill or left.

Evaluation

While voluntary projects are different from statutory agencies, both must be accountable to their users and to their paymasters for the service they provide. Provision of a good service must be the main justification for any project and proper methods of evaluation should be incorporated in the planning. Evaluation should not be seen solely in numerical terms, but in the quality of the service as perceived by the providers and more so, perhaps, by the users. The voluntary sector is continually under threat from lack of funding. It has considerable strengths and resilience but must, despite its funding problems, uphold the standards it seeks in theory by the practice it employs.

Conclusions

Voluntary agencies have a valuable role to play but they can never be the sole, or indeed the central, providers of housing. This is clearly the responsibility of housing authorities within local councils. Voluntary agencies wish to see local authorities take up their responsibility for young people, as is being done in some areas, so that provision can be coordinated and comprehensive. Such provision should include direct-access emergency accommodation for as long as necessary; hostels for those who desire communal living and a substantial amount of support; and a range of other accommodation, both furnished and unfurnished, including bedsits, flats and shared housing. Some voluntary agencies are already developing these in their own work. Voluntary organisations are best qualified to introduce innovative approaches, test out new methods on a small scale, develop techniques which can be generally applied and then offer successful models to authorities.

Voluntary organisations working in partnership with central and/or local government will be more effective than working in isolation and will usefully complement statutory provision. Through co-operation in determining needs and ensuring they are met in appropriate ways, central government support, and particularly DHSS funds, will be more effectively and more economically used than on bed-and-breakfast accommodation. Housing provision must, however, be part of a comprehensive strategy for youth and the voluntary sector cannot provide this alone. Good housing is the base from which employment, education and other opportunities stem.

11
RECOMMENDATIONS

1   That statutory and voluntary agencies, working in partnership, should develop a comprehensive strategy to alleviate the problem of homelessness among young people. This should facilitate the development of a range of services including direct-access emergency accommodation, hostels, bed-sits, flats and houses.

2   That during the International Year of Shelter for the Homeless (1987) HM Government should show its commitment to homeless young people by increasing expenditure from public funds and providing more financial and practical assistance to voluntary organisations concerned with the young homeless.

3   That HM Government should strengthen the Housing Act 1985 (Part III) for England and Wales and the Housing (Homeless Persons) Act (1977) for Scotland so that a mandatory responsibility is placed on local authorities to secure accommodation for all homeless people.

4   That HM Government and local authorities should immediately undertake the collection of data, so that the numbers of homeless young people can be accurately assessed and constructive planning begin.

5   That the DES should devise a means of including the subject of 'leaving home' within school pro-

grammes and in particular for those preparing to leave school.

6 That the DHSS should withdraw the regulations which limit the length of time during which a young person living in a particular place may receive Board and Lodging payments.

7 That local authorities should review their policies toward housing young people from care and ensure that adequate support systems are set up to ease their transition to independent living.

8 That sufficient capital funding be made available to enable voluntary organisations to replace outdated facilities, the resources released by closing worn-out accommodation being used to develop new initiatives, including small-scale projects.

9 That agencies, statutory and voluntary, should place greater emphasis on the employment and training needs of young people.

10 That adequate accommodation as well as medical and counselling services should be provided, as a matter of urgency, for those young people with drug and alcohol related problems who are at present forced to live on the streets or in bed-and-breakfast accommodation.

11 That the voluntary sector review its policies toward ethnic minorities and take action to develop a truly equal opportunities policy for housing young people from those groups.

12 That voluntary organisations make every effort to improve the co-ordination of services for young people and that informal networks be set up country-wide.

APPENDIX 1
Select List of Organisations and Projects Contacted

Alone in London Service
Anti-Slavery Society
Blue Triangle, Glasgow
Bosco House Children's Home, Glasgow (now closed)
Bridges Project, Hatfield
Bury Project, Greater Manchester
Centrepoint, Soho, London
CHAR, The Housing Campaign for Single Homeless People, London
Children's Society, London
— Central London Teenage Project
— Independence Project, Walsall
Crisis at Christmas
Cyrenians, Cambridge
First Key, London
Glasgow Council for the Single Homeless (GCSH)
Glasgow Housing Authority
Glengowan Hostel, Glasgow
Great Chapel Street Medical Centre, London
Hungerford Drug Project, London
Housing Aid Centre, Manchester
Manchester Single Person's Team, Housing Department
Kaleidoscope Youth and Community Project, Kingston-upon-Thames
Leaving Home Project, London
Longstop Project Ltd, Lewisham, London
National Association of Young People in Care (NAYPIC)
— Bradford and London
National Children's Home, London

— NCH Independence Training Unit, Elmstead Woods, Surrey
National Federation of Housing Associations
National Association of Probation Officers
New Horizon Youth Centre, London
North Lambeth Day Centre, London
Open Door Project, Livingston, Scotland
Piccadilly Advice Centre (PAC), London
Signpost Youth Advice Centre, Wythenshawe, Manchester
Salvation Army —
259 Project, London
— Midnight Patrol, London
Scottish Council for Single Homeless (SCSH), Edinburgh
Shades, Manchester
Shelter, London and Edinburgh
Short-Stay Young Homeless Project, Bina Gardens, London
Soho Project, London
Stopover, Edinburgh
Stopover, Manchester
Streetwise International, Cambridge
UJIMA Housing Association, London
UK Committee for UNICEF, London
Young Homelessness Group, London
West End Co-ordinated Voluntary Service (WECVS), London

APPENDIX 2
Brief Details of
Projects Visited

Alone in London Service
West Lodge, 190 Euston Road, London NW1 2EF. Tel: 01–
387 6184

An advice and counselling service for young people aged 16–
25 who are homeless and at risk in London. The organisation
runs a 21-bed long-stay supportive hostel with on-site education and training opportunities to help people to move on to
independent living. A 6-bed (unsupported) shared house is
also available.

Bina Gardens
See *Short-Stay Young Homeless Project*

Blue Triangle
Dorothy McCall House, 2 Somerset Place, Charing Cross,
Glasgow G3 7JT. Tel: (041) 332 8365

A hostel run by Glasgow Young Women's Christian
Association. It offers supported accommodation in shared
rooms for girls over 16 who are not ready to live independently. Practical help and activities programmes are
available.

Bridges Project (NCH)
9b St Albans Road East, Hatfield, Herts. Tel: (070 72) 66834

A project incorporating day centre facilities, sports and social
activities, advice and information for young people, and a
'crash pad' which offers emergency accommodation for
homeless young people. The project has strong community
links and contacts with long-stay and permanent accommodation through housing associations and other agencies.

Central London Teenage Project

c/o The Children's Society, 91–93 Queens Road, London SE15 2EZ. Tel: 01–639 1466.

A safe house for up to 12 teenagers who have run away from home or care and found their way to London. It is the first such project in the UK. It tries to gain the trust of young people and encourage them, parents, and social workers to communicate so as to find acceptable accommodation for the residents. A three-year research programme is being undertaken to establish the number of young people who run away to London and their reasons for doing so.

Centrepoint, Soho

33 Long Acre, London WC2E 9LA. Tel: 01–379 3466

An emergency night shelter for young people aged 16–19 situated in the West End of London. Accommodation is in separate men's and women's dormitories in a church crypt. Overnight accommodation, breakfast, evening meal and counselling facilities are available. Open 8 p.m.–8 a.m., every night. Takes maximum of 32 people. It also manages a long-stay hostel in Hammersmith and flats throughout London.

CHAR

The Housing Campaign for Single Homeless People, 5–15 Cromer Street, London WC1H 8LS. Tel: 01–833 2071

Originally known as the Campaign for the Homeless and Rootless, CHAR represents 280 organisations and more than 200 individuals who provide services for single homeless people. Its role is threefold:

● to inform, by publishing guides on the rights of people without a home;

● to represent the views of those who provide services to homeless people;

● to campaign for the rights of single people to a home of their own, expose the squalid condition in which many thousands of single people are forced to live and press government for the resources to provide an adequate standard of housing.

Local groups discuss common experiences and possible solutions.

Cyrenians
4 Short Street, Cambridge CB1 1LB. Tel: (0223) 67797

Provides a 'drop-in' bus which acts as a day centre for homeless people in the centre of the city. While it was originally set up to meet the needs of older homeless people, the bus with its coffee, sandwiches and social support is increasingly used by young homeless people. Informal advice and counselling are available and the project, funded and partially run by the local authority, has good links with other statutory and voluntary services.

Glasgow Council for Single Homeless (GCSH)
c/o Single Persons Section, Lomond House, Glasgow District Council, 9 George Square, Glasgow G2 1TG. Tel: (041) 227 4219

A group of organisations concerned with the housing provision for homeless single people in Glasgow. The group have a close working relationship with Glasgow Housing Department and monitor housing provision and policies in the city. A report *Rehousing Hostel Residents: Experience in Glasgow* (1985) looked at recent experience in the city.

Glengowan Hostel
196 Nithsdale Road, Pollokshields, Glasgow G41 1TU. Tel: (041) 424 1246

A supportive hostel for homeless young men aged 16–21 offering accommodation and skills training.

Great Chapel Street Medical Centre
13 Great Chapel Street, London W1V 7AL. Tel: 01–437 9360

Offers primary health care to homeless people in London at a 'walk-in' centre. Staff have considerable experience in caring for the homeless and offer chiropody, psychiatric and counselling services.

Hungerford Drug Project
26 Craven Street, London WC2N 5NT. Tel: 01–930 4688

A street-based agency providing information, advice, referral and counselling services to drug users, their families and friends in London. Some detached work is carried out in the area.

Kaleidoscope Youth and Community Project
40–46 Cromwell Road, Kingston-upon-Thames, Surrey KT2
6RE. Tel: 01–549 2681

A project incorporating an all-night youth club, hostel, medical and educational facilities for young people, many of whom are homeless. It is also the drug dependency unit for south-west London and specialises in problems of drug misuse.

Leaving Home Project
5 Egmont House, 116 Shaftesbury Avenue, London W1V
7DJ. Tel: 01–437 2068

An educational project which encourages teachers and youth workers to raise the issues of leaving home and homelessness in their teaching by offering advice and training. It is evaluating some resources currently available to teachers and how they are used in practice. Also has an advisory role for people designing resources and assesses the feasibility of new resources.

Longstop Project Ltd
300a Stanstead Road, London SE23 1DE. Tel: 01–699
4141

Offers housing for single homeless young people in seven houses in London. Longstop aims to develop an innovative style of management for young people's housing. A high degree of support and advice is offered since the majority of residents are unemployed.

National Association of Young People in Care (NAYPIC)
2nd Floor, Wool Exchange, Market Street, Bradford BD1
1LD. Tel: (0274) 728484
London Office: 20 Compton Terrace, London N1 2UN. Tel:
01–226 7102

A national organisation set up by and for young people who have been, or are, in care. It seeks to highlight the views of this group of young people, to inform them of their rights, to draw attention to their needs and campaign for changes in legislation and practices which are perceived to be detrimental. The Royal Jubilee Trust has grant-aided a survey of the problems facing young people leaving care.

National Children's Home (NCH)
85 Highbury Park, London N5 1UD. Tel: 01–226 2033

NCH was set up by the Methodist Church in 1869 and has traditionally provided residential Children's Homes. Emphasis in recent years has changed. Large residential homes are closing and family support through family centres, phone-in services and counselling is taking their place. NCH is pioneering a number of innovatory projects, such as the independence training units for young people from care. It has also successfully highlighted the threats facing children from drugs, drink, divorce, disability and abuse through its 'Children in Danger' campaign.

NCH Elmstead Woods Project
Surrey (now closed)

An independence training unit for young people from care. See also *Bridges*.

New Horizon Youth Centre
1 Macklin Street, London WC2B 5NH. Tel: 01–242 0010

The Centre offers a day centre predominantly for homeless people under 21, housing advice and access to permanent accommodation. Activities range from pool tables to music, art or discussion groups and sessions on making videos. Individual members also campaign on housing issues.

North Lambeth Day Centre
St John's Crypt, 73 Waterloo Road, London SE1 8UD. Tel: 01–261 9622

A non-residential centre for single homeless men and women. It is open in the afternoons, Monday to Friday, on a drop-in basis and in the morning for those who wish to make particular use of services. NLDC offers social work support/counselling, access to health care groups, advice and advocacy, activities such as an art room and workshop, laundry and washing facilities. The day centre is linked with an adult literacy and basic skills development scheme; a housing support team to help those moving into independent housing; and four residential houses.

Open Door Project
c/o 98 Kenilworth Rise, Dedridge, Livingston, Scotland EH54 6JL. Tel: (0506) 412205

A voluntary organisation which has recently set up a hostel offering direct access emergency accommodation for young people in Livingston. The project is based on thorough research into needs.

Piccadilly Advice Centre
100 Shaftesbury Avenue, London W1V 7DH. Tel: 01–437 1579 (Admin.); 01–434 3773 (Advice)

An independent advice centre offering housing and welfare rights advice to young homeless people in the West End of London and those new to London.

Salvation Army 259 Project
Waterloo Road, London SE1. Tel: 01–269 0029

Provides supported accommodation in self-catering bed-sits for young men. Up to 12 youths are accommodated for up to one year before being resettled permanently.

Salvation Army Midnight Patrol
11 Argyll Street, London WC1H 8EJ. Tel: 01–837 5149

Overnight accommodation is provided for one night for youngsters left temporarily homeless at Euston, St Pancras, King's Cross and Paddington stations. The workers are out on the stations every night and befriend those left homeless.

Scottish Council for Single Homeless (SCSH)
4 Old Assembly Close, Edinburgh EH1 1QX Tel: (031) 226 4382

An umbrella body bringing together a range of voluntary and statutory organisations concerned to campaign for proper housing for single people. The Council conducts research, publishes reports and prepares policy statements designed to highlight the needs of single homeless people and the action necessary to improve the range of housing options and the quality of provision for them.

Shades City Centre Project
48a Copperas Street, Manchester M4 1HS. Tel: (061) 834 7360

A youth work project with young people aged 16–26, who are leaving or changing home. The project provides information, advice and counselling on all issues affecting young people, especially on housing, social services and the law. It provides a free pregnancy testing service, and is open Monday to Friday mornings (10 a.m.–1 p.m.) and Monday to Wednesday evenings (7–9 p.m.). The project has access to limited emergency accommodation and liaises with longer-term provision. It also campaigns to improve provision for the young homeless, using direct action methods.

Shelter
The National Campaign for the Homeless, 157 Waterloo Road, London SE1 8XF. Tel: 01–633 9377

Offers help and advice to homeless people and campaigns to reduce the scandal of increasing homelessness. Shelter funds more than 25 housing aid centres which offer assistance to homeless people and those who are badly housed. A variety of housing projects have been set up and sponsored by Shelter to test new ideas and show what can be done. Shelter provides information and briefings to Members of Parliament, the press and broadcasters and the general public. Local groups highlight local needs and inform the public on national priorities.

Shelter
Scottish Campaign for the Homeless, 65 Cockburn Street, Edinburgh EH1 1BU. Tel: (031) 226 6347

Set up in 1968 to try to eradicate homelessness and bad housing in Scotland. A number of projects have been set up to bring empty houses into use in rural areas and increase the housing opportunities for young people. Shelter runs three housing aid centres and employs a special young persons housing worker.

Short-Stay Young Homeless Project (Bina Gardens)
4 Bina Gardens, London SW5 0LA. Tel: 01–373 0635

A hostel offering 27 people up to four weeks' supported accommodation in shared rooms. The rent includes half board during the week and full board at weekends. The property is owned by the Threshold Housing Association and managed by a group of voluntary organisations in the West End Network, who set up the project in 1979. The project also manages a second-stage hostel and cluster flats in Holloway Road, London, to help young people in transition from the short-stay hostel to independent living.

Stopover
9 Mayfield Gardens, Edinburgh EH9 2AX. Tel: (031) 667 2763

A short-stay hostel run by the Edinburgh Council for the Single Homeless to provide emergency accommodation for young homeless people aged 16–21.

Stopover
8 Scarsdale Road, Victoria Park, Manchester M14 5RS. Tel: (061) 224 8594

A short-stay hostel for young women aged 16–21 requiring substantial support and assistance before establishing an independent lifestyle.

UJIMA Housing Association
413–419 Harrow Road, London W9 3QJ. Tel: 01–969 9690

Offers accommodation in flats, bed-sits and converted houses for black young people in London. There is limited support and residents must be able to live independently, although intensive management skills are used.

Young Homelessness Group
c/o CHAR, 5–15 Cromer Street, London WC1 8LS. Tel: 01–833 2071

A co-ordinating group which looks at the issues affecting young homeless people. It includes a broad range of voluntary agencies which seek to encourage a wide debate on leaving home.

West End Co-ordinated Voluntary Service (WECVS)
54–56 New Oxford Street, London WC1A 1ES. Tel: 01–580 2808

A co-ordinating body for voluntary agencies working with the single homeless in the West End of London. The agencies in membership aim to offer a comprehensive service for the homeless in the city.

APPENDIX 3
Further Reading

DEARLING, A. AND CLARK, M. *Leaving Home*: A training manual for workers with young people. Scots Group/Intermediate Treatment Resource Centre, 1985, £1.00.

LEAVING HOME PROJECT *Finding Out About Housing – A List of Resources*, 3rd edition, 1984, £1.00.

NATIONAL FEDERATION OF HOUSING ASSOCIATIONS *A Guide for Housing Associations Working with Voluntary Organisations*. Special Project Guide No. 2, 3rd Edition 1984, £1.00.

PICCADILLY ADVICE CENTRE *Bored with Lodging*: A report on the effects of the new board and lodging regulations, May/June 1985.

SCOTTISH COUNCIL FOR SINGLE HOMELESS
Alternatives to Night Shelters, January 1984, £2.00 plus postage.
Think Single, May 1981, £2.50 plus postage.
Hostel Funding by Alan D. K. Logan, January 1985, £2.50 plus postage.
Opening Doors: A report on allocating houses to single people, March 1984, £2.00 plus postage.

SHADES CITY CENTRE PROJECT *Manchester Survival Guide*, 1984, £1.00.

SHELTER (Scotland) *Homeless Young People in Glasgow*, September 1984, £2.00.